CANON EOS R7 USER MANUAL

The Photographer's Handbook to Get the Best from this Popular Mirrorless Camera

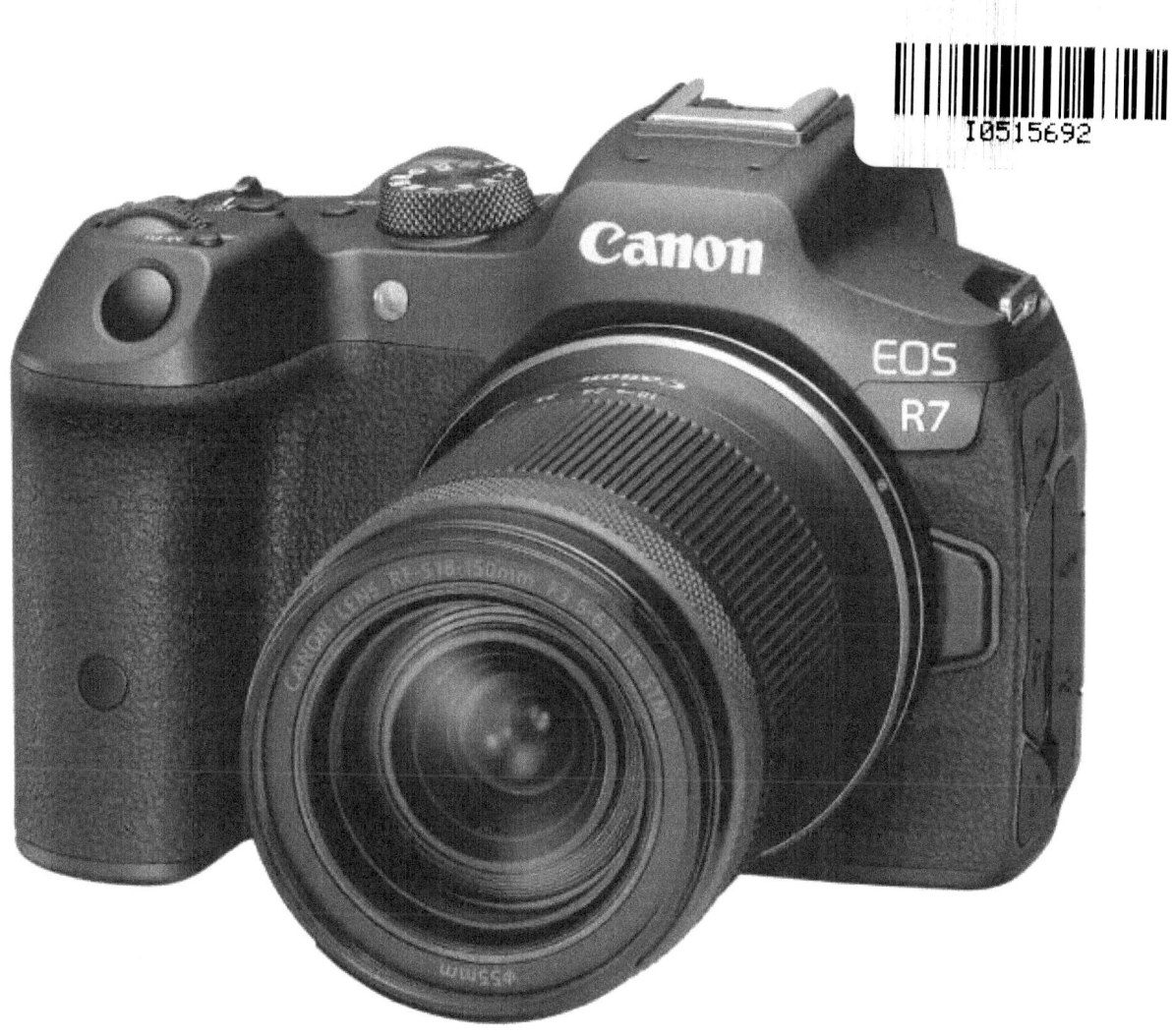

JEFF M. SATTERFIELD

Copyright © 2024 Jeff M. Satterfield

Unauthorized reproduction, distribution, or transmission of any part of this publication in any form or by any means, including photocopying, recording, or other electronic or mechanical methods, without the prior written permission of the publisher, is prohibited.
Brief quotations may be used in critical reviews and other non-commercial uses permitted by copyright law, provided proper attribution is given.

TABLE OF CONTENTS

DISCLAIMER 6
CHAPTER ONE 8
   INTRODUCTION 8
      Overview of the Canon EOS R7 8
      Key Features: 8
      What's in the Box? 10
CHAPTER TWO 12
   GETTING STARTED WITH CANON EOS R7 12
      Unboxing and First Impressions 12
      Charging the Battery and Setup 13
      Camera Layout and Button Overview 15
      Navigating the Menu System 18
CHAPTER THREE 22
   CANON EOS R7'S IMAGING SYSTEM 22
      APS-C Sensor and Image Processor 22
      Dual Pixel Autofocus Technology 23
      Image Quality and Resolution 25
      ISO Sensitivity Range 28
CHAPTER FOUR 30
   LENS AND ACCCESSORIES 30
      Compatible RF and EF Lenses 30
      Adapters for EF Lenses 32
      Essential Accessories (Batteries, Memory Cards, Grips) 34
CHAPTER FIVE 38
   MASTERING CAMERA MODES 38
      Auto Mode and Scene Modes 38
      Manual Mode (M) 40
      Aperture Priority (Av) 42
      Shutter Priority (Tv) 44
      Program Mode (P) 47
CHAPTER SIX 50
   AUTOFOCUS AND TRACKING SYSTEMS 50
      AF Modes and Functions 50

Face and Eye Detection 53

Subject Tracking Features 55

Customizing Autofocus Settings 57

CHAPTER SEVEN 62

SHOOTING STILL PHOTOS 62

Shooting in RAW vs JPEG 62

Burst Shooting and Continuous Mode 64

Using the Electronic Shutter 67

Understanding Exposure (ISO, Aperture, Shutter Speed) 69

CHAPTER EIGHT 74

SHOOTING VIDEOS 74

Video Recording Options 74

4K Video and Frame Rates 76

Autofocus for Video Recording 78

Stabilization Features for Smooth Video 81

CHAPTER NINE 84

ADVANCED FEATURES OF CANON EOS R7 84

In-Body Image Stabilization (IBIS) 84

Dual Pixel RAW 86

High-Speed Shooting 88

Customizable Function Buttons 90

CHAPTER TEN 94

CONNECTIVITY AND SHARING OPTIONS 94

Wi-Fi and Bluetooth Setup 94

Connecting to Smartphones (Canon Camera Connect App) 96

File Transfer and Remote Shooting 99

CHAPTER ELEVEN 104

MAINTENANCE AND TROUBLESHOOTING 104

Cleaning the Camera Sensor and Lenses 104

Firmware Updates 107

Common Errors and How to Fix Them 109

CHAPTER TWELVE 114

TIPS AND TRICKS FOR BETTER PHOTOGRAPHY 114

Shooting in Low Light Conditions 114

Using Filters and Effects 116

Composing Shots with the Rule of Thirds 119
Mastering Portraits, Landscapes, and Macro Photography 121

DISCLAIMER

The contents of this book are provided for informational and entertainment purposes only. The author and publisher do not make any representations or warranties regarding the accuracy, applicability, completeness, or suitability of the contents for any purpose.

The information in this book is based on the author's personal experiences, research, and opinions, and should not be considered a substitute for professional advice. Readers are advised to consult appropriate professionals regarding their specific situations.

The author and publisher are not liable for any loss, injury, or damage allegedly arising from the information or suggestions in this book. Any reliance on such information is at the reader's own risk.

The inclusion of third-party resources, websites, or references does not imply endorsement or responsibility for their content or services.

Readers are encouraged to use their own discretion and judgment when applying the information or recommendations in this book to their own lives.

All rights reserved. No part of this book may be reproduced, distributed, or transmitted in any form or by any means without the prior written permission of the publisher, except for brief quotations in critical reviews and certain other non-commercial uses permitted by copyright law.

Thank you for reading and understanding this disclaimer.

CHAPTER ONE
INTRODUCTION

Overview of the Canon EOS R7

The Canon EOS R7 is a versatile and advanced mirrorless camera designed for both enthusiasts and professionals. Launched as part of Canon's R series, it combines cutting-edge technology with an ergonomic design, making it suitable for a wide range of photography styles, including wildlife, sports, portraits, and landscapes.

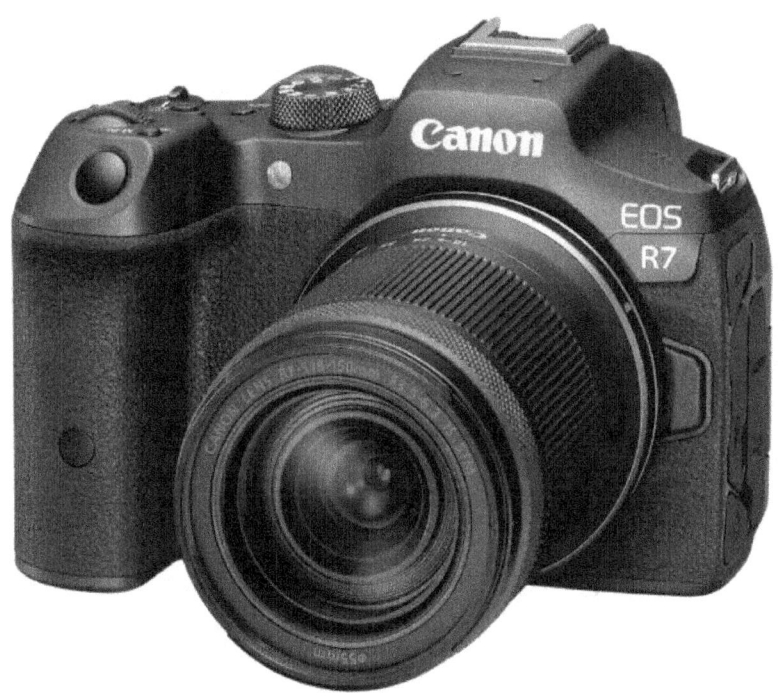

Key Features:

1. **Sensor and Image Quality**:

   o The EOS R7 is equipped with a 32.5-megapixel APS-C CMOS sensor that delivers stunning image quality with excellent detail and dynamic range.

   o It features Dual Pixel CMOS AF II technology, providing fast and accurate autofocus performance across a wide area of the frame.

2. **Continuous Shooting**:

   o The camera offers impressive continuous shooting capabilities, allowing photographers to capture up to 30 frames per second (fps) with the electronic shutter, making it ideal for action photography.

3. **In-Body Image Stabilization (IBIS)**:

   o The EOS R7 includes a sophisticated in-body stabilization system that helps reduce camera shake, enabling smoother handheld shots and improved low-light performance.

4. **Video Capabilities**:

- The R7 supports 4K video recording at up to 60 fps and Full HD recording at up to 120 fps, catering to videographers seeking high-quality video capture with advanced autofocus features.

5. **Connectivity Options**:
    - The camera is equipped with built-in Wi-Fi and Bluetooth, allowing for seamless connectivity to smartphones and other devices for remote shooting and easy file sharing.

6. **Vari-Angle Touchscreen LCD**:
    - The 3.0-inch vari-angle touchscreen LCD provides flexibility in composing shots from different angles, making it a valuable feature for vloggers and creative photographers.

7. **Weather-Sealed Body**:
    - The EOS R7 features a durable, weather-sealed body that enhances its reliability in various shooting conditions, making it suitable for outdoor photography.

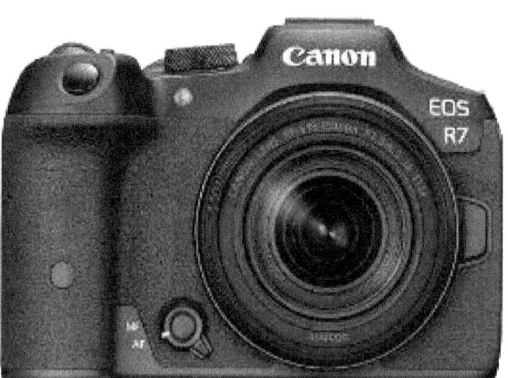

8. **Extensive Lens Compatibility**:
    - As part of the Canon R system, the EOS R7 is compatible with a wide range of RF lenses and can also utilize EF lenses with an adapter, offering versatility in lens choices.

The Canon EOS R7 stands out as a powerful tool for photographers and videographers, combining high-resolution imaging, fast performance, and robust features in a compact design. Its advanced capabilities cater to a variety of photographic genres, making it an excellent choice for both aspiring and experienced creators looking to elevate their craft.

What's in the Box?

When you purchase the **Canon EOS R7**, the package typically includes the following items:

1. **Canon EOS R7 Camera Body**
   - The main unit of the camera with an ergonomic design for comfortable handling.

2. **Canon RF-S 18-150mm f/3.5-6.3 IS STM Lens** (if included in the kit)
   - A versatile zoom lens suitable for various photography styles, from wide-angle to portrait.

3. **Battery Pack (LP-E6NH)**
   - A rechargeable lithium-ion battery providing power to the camera.

4. **Battery Charger (LC-E6)**
   - A charger for recharging the battery.

5. **Camera Strap**
   - A comfortable strap for carrying the camera.

6. **USB Cable**
   - A cable for connecting the camera to a computer or compatible device for data transfer.

7. **User Manual**
   - A detailed guide providing information on camera features, settings, and operation.

8. **Warranty Card**
   - A card outlining warranty information and conditions for the camera.

9. **Software CD or Download Information**
   - Access to Canon's software for photo editing and camera management (often available for download).

10. **Eyecup**
    - An accessory that fits into the viewfinder area to block light and provide comfort when shooting.

Note: The contents may vary based on the specific kit or bundle purchased. It's always a good idea to check the packaging or retailer's description for any additional accessories that may be included.

CHAPTER TWO
GETTING STARTED WITH CANON EOS R7

Unboxing and First Impressions

Unboxing the Canon EOS R7 is an exciting experience, especially for photography enthusiasts eager to explore its features. Here's a breakdown of the unboxing process and the initial impressions one might have:

Unboxing Experience

1. **Packaging**:
   - The Canon EOS R7 comes in a sturdy and visually appealing box, with images of the camera prominently displayed. The packaging is designed to protect the contents during transit, ensuring everything arrives in perfect condition.

2. **Opening the Box**:
   - As you open the box, the first thing you notice is the careful arrangement of the items, each section holding specific components securely. This thoughtful design minimizes the risk of damage.

3. **Contents**:
   - Lifting the lid reveals the camera body, typically wrapped in protective material to prevent scratches and impact damage. Underneath, you will find the lens (if included), battery, charger, strap, cables, and manuals neatly packaged.

First Impressions

1. **Build Quality**:
   - The EOS R7 has a robust and well-constructed body. The materials used feel premium, giving a solid first impression. The weather-sealed design reassures users about its durability, especially in challenging shooting conditions.

2. **Ergonomics**:
   - The camera is designed for comfort, with a grip that fits well in the hand. The placement of buttons and dials feels intuitive, making it easy to navigate settings and functions without taking your eye off the viewfinder.

3. **Weight and Size**:
   - The EOS R7 strikes a balance between being compact and lightweight, making it suitable for extended shooting sessions without causing fatigue. Despite its smaller size compared to full-frame cameras, it does not compromise on functionality.

4. **Display and Viewfinder**:
   - The vari-angle touchscreen LCD is a standout feature, providing flexibility for composing shots at various angles. The screen is bright and responsive, making

it easy to adjust settings and review images. The electronic viewfinder (EVF) is clear and offers a high refresh rate, which enhances the shooting experience.

5. **Initial Setup**:
   - Setting up the camera for the first time is straightforward, with a user-friendly menu system that guides you through the initial configurations. Connecting the camera to a smartphone via Wi-Fi or Bluetooth for remote control is also simple, enhancing connectivity right from the start.

6. **Performance**:
   - Upon powering on the camera, the startup time is quick, and the autofocus system feels remarkably fast and accurate. The initial shots taken highlight the camera's impressive image quality, with vibrant colours and sharp details.

Overall, the unboxing experience of the Canon EOS R7 is both thrilling and satisfying. The camera's build quality, ergonomics, and advanced features create a positive first impression, setting the stage for an enjoyable and productive photography journey. Whether you are a seasoned professional or an enthusiastic beginner, the EOS R7 promises to be a reliable companion in capturing stunning images and videos.

Charging the Battery and Setup

Charging the battery and setting up your Canon EOS R7 is a crucial first step before you start shooting. Here's a guide to help you through the process:

Charging the Battery

1. **Locate the Battery**:
   - Remove the battery from the camera body. To do this, open the battery compartment located at the bottom of the camera. Press the battery release latch to unlock it, then slide the battery out.

2. **Insert the Battery into the Charger**:
   - Take the included battery charger (LC-E6) and insert the battery (LP-E6NH) into the charger. Make sure it fits securely, aligning the contacts on the battery with the contacts in the charger.

3. **Plug in the Charger**:
   - Connect the charger to a power outlet using the provided power cable. The charger usually has an indicator light that shows the charging status:
     - **Red Light**: Indicates that the battery is charging.
     - **Green Light**: Indicates that the battery is fully charged.

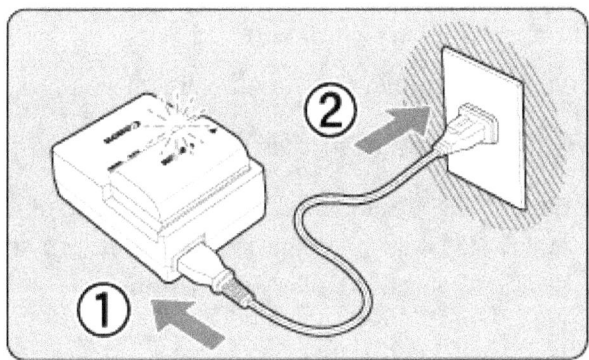

4. **Charging Time**:
   - It typically takes about 2 to 3 hours to fully charge the battery. Once charged, unplug the charger and remove the battery.

Setting Up the Canon EOS R7

1. **Inserting the Battery**:
   - Insert the charged battery back into the camera. Ensure it's inserted correctly, with the battery contacts facing the appropriate direction. Close the battery compartment securely.

2. **Inserting a Memory Card**:
   - Open the memory card slot cover on the side of the camera. Insert an SD card (compatible with UHS-II for best performance) into the slot until it clicks into place. Close the memory card slot cover.

3. **Powering On the Camera**:
   - Turn the power switch (located on the top right of the camera body) to the "ON" position. The camera will initialize, and you'll see the Canon logo on the LCD screen.

4. **Setting the Date and Time**:
   - After powering on, you'll be prompted to set the date, time, and time zone. Use the touchscreen to navigate through the settings and input the correct information.

5. **Selecting Language**:
   - Choose your preferred language from the menu options. This will set the language for the camera's menu system.

6. **Customizing Settings**:
   - The EOS R7 offers a variety of customizable settings to tailor the camera to your shooting preferences. Explore the menu system to adjust:
     - Image quality (RAW or JPEG)
     - Autofocus settings

- Display options
- Drive mode (single, continuous, timer)

7. **Connecting to Wi-Fi/Bluetooth (Optional)**:
   - If you want to connect your camera to a smartphone or other devices for remote control or image transfer, go to the **Wi-Fi/Bluetooth settings** in the menu and follow the prompts to establish the connection.

8. **Familiarizing Yourself with Controls**:
   - Take a moment to familiarize yourself with the layout of buttons and dials. Understanding their functions will help you navigate the camera more efficiently while shooting.

Charging the battery and setting up your Canon EOS R7 is a straightforward process that prepares you for capturing stunning photos and videos. Once everything is set up, take some time to explore the camera's features and practice shooting in different modes to get the most out of your new gear.

Camera Layout and Button Overview

The Canon EOS R7 features an intuitive layout and a variety of buttons designed for easy access to essential functions. Here's a detailed overview of the camera's layout and the functions of its key buttons:

1. Top View

- **Mode Dial**:
  - Located on the left side, this dial allows you to select different shooting modes, including Auto, Manual (M), Aperture Priority (Av), Shutter Priority (Tv), and Scene Modes.

- **Shutter Button**:
  - The main button for capturing photos. It is typically located on the right side of the camera, above the grip.

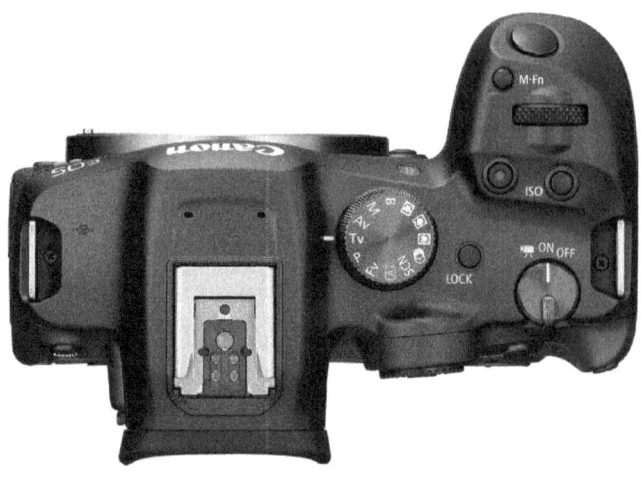

- **Power Switch**:
    - o Located around the shutter button, this switch turns the camera on and off.
- **Exposure Compensation Dial**:
    - o This dial allows you to quickly adjust exposure compensation for brighter or darker images.
- **Hot Shoe**:
    - o Positioned above the viewfinder, this shoe allows you to attach external flash units or accessories.

2. Back View

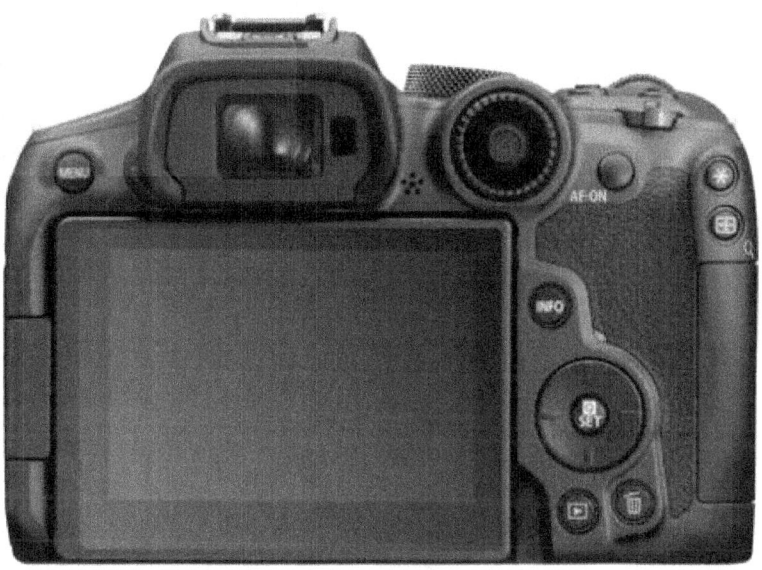

- **Vari-Angle Touchscreen LCD**:
    - o A 3.0-inch LCD that can be tilted and rotated for easy viewing from different angles. It's touch-sensitive, allowing for intuitive navigation and focus selection.
- **Viewfinder (EVF)**:
    - o An electronic viewfinder located above the LCD screen, providing a high-resolution view of your composition and settings.
- **Multi-Function Button**:
    - o This customizable button can be programmed to access frequently used functions, such as changing autofocus modes or settings.
- **Menu Button**:
    - o Opens the camera's main menu for accessing settings and configurations.

- **Playback Button**:
    - Allows you to view your captured images and videos.
- **Info Button**:
    - Toggles the information display on the screen, showing or hiding shooting information and settings.
- **Quick Control Button**:
    - Provides quick access to commonly used settings, allowing for faster adjustments without going through the full menu.

3. Side View

- **Memory Card Slot**:
    - Located on the left side, this slot accommodates an SD card. It typically has a cover that opens for easy access.

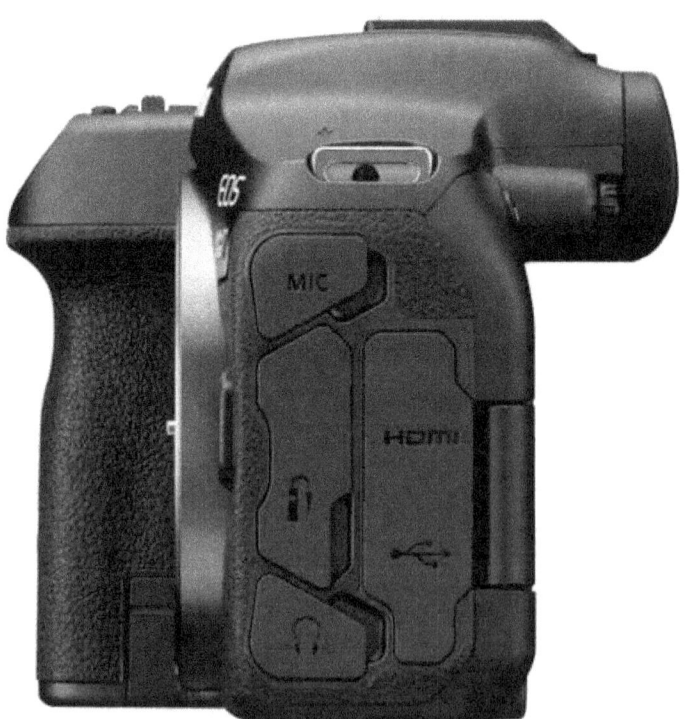

- **Connectivity Ports**:
    - **USB-C Port**: Used for connecting to a computer or charger.
    - **HDMI Port**: For connecting to external monitors or devices.
    - **Microphone Input**: For connecting external microphones for better audio quality in video recording.
    - **Headphone Jack**: For monitoring audio during video recording.

4. **Front View**

- **Lens Mount**:
    - The RF lens mount allows you to attach Canon RF lenses, providing a wide range of photographic options.

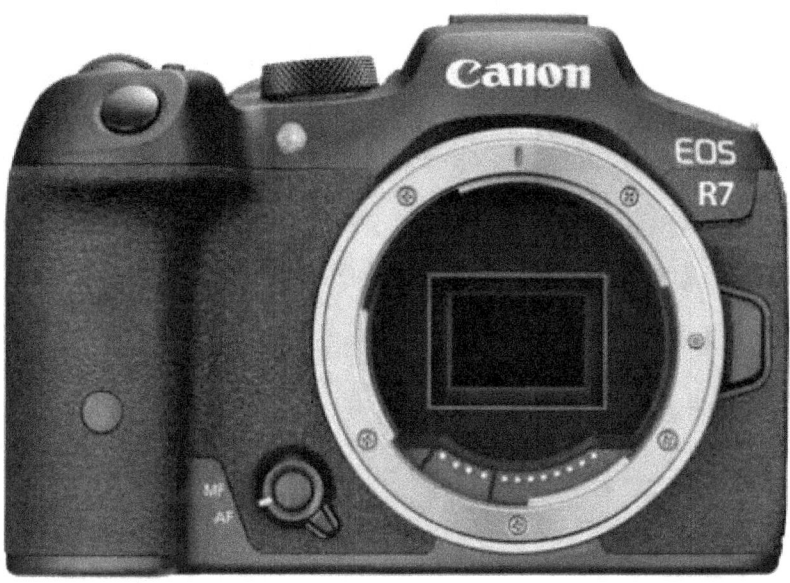

- **AF Assist Beam**:
    - A small light that helps with autofocus in low-light situations, usually located near the lens mount.
- **Depth of Field Preview Button**:
    - This button, typically found near the lens mount, allows you to preview the depth of field in the shot before capturing it.

Understanding the layout and functionality of the Canon EOS R7's buttons and controls is essential for maximizing your shooting experience. Familiarizing yourself with these features will help you navigate the camera quickly and efficiently, allowing you to focus on capturing stunning images and videos. Take some time to explore the buttons and practice using them to develop a comfortable workflow!

Navigating the Menu System

The Canon EOS R7 features a user-friendly menu system that provides access to various camera settings and functions. Here's a guide on how to navigate the menu effectively:

1. **Accessing the Menu**

- **Menu Button**:
    - Press the **Menu** button located on the back of the camera to open the main menu screen.

2. Understanding the Menu Structure

The menu is organized into several tabs, each containing specific settings. Here's a breakdown of the main tabs you'll encounter:

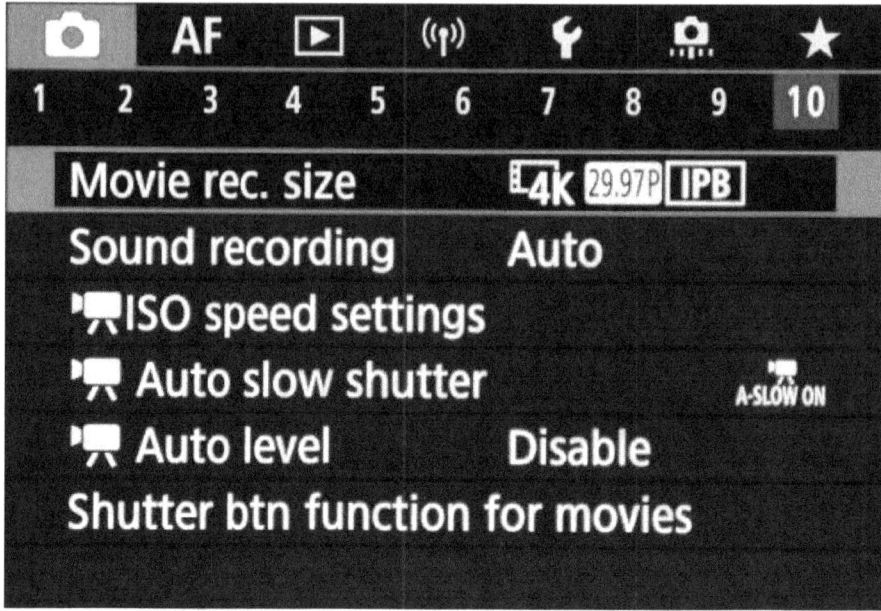

- **Shooting Menu (Red Tab)**:
    - This menu includes options related to shooting settings, such as image quality, autofocus settings, metering modes, drive modes, and more.

- **Playback Menu (Yellow Tab)**:
    - Here, you can find options for reviewing images, deleting files, and accessing playback settings.

- **Setup Menu (Blue Tab)**:
    - This menu allows you to configure various camera settings, including date and time, language, and custom functions. It also contains connectivity settings for Wi-Fi and Bluetooth.

- **Custom Functions (Orange Tab)**:
    - This section provides options to customize the camera's behaviour to suit your shooting style. You can adjust settings for buttons, autofocus, and more.

- **My Menu (Star Tab)**:
    - This is a customizable menu where you can add frequently used settings for quick access. It's useful for streamlining your workflow.

3. Navigating the Menu

- **Using the Touchscreen**:

- The EOS R7's touchscreen allows for intuitive navigation. Simply swipe and tap to move through the menus and select options. Use your finger to scroll through the list of settings or swipe between tabs.
- **Using the Multi-Function Control Dial**:
  - You can also navigate the menu using the **Multi-Function Control Dial** located on the back of the camera. Rotate the dial to scroll through options and press the centre button to select an item.
- **Using the Arrow Keys**:
  - The arrow keys (if available) on the back of the camera can be used to navigate through the menu options. Use the up/down/left/right arrows to move through the settings.

4. Adjusting Settings

- **Selecting a Setting**:
  - Once you navigate to a specific setting, press the **Set** button (usually in the centre of the Multi-Function Control Dial) to open options for that setting.
- **Changing Values**:
  - For settings that require adjustments (e.g., exposure compensation, ISO), use the touchscreen or the dial to change the values. Press **Set** to confirm your selection.

5. Exiting the Menu

- To exit the menu, you can press the **Menu** button again or simply tap outside the menu area on the touchscreen. This will return you to the live view or shooting mode.

6. Tips for Efficient Menu Navigation

- **Familiarize Yourself with Tabs**: Take time to explore each tab in the menu to understand where specific settings are located.
- **Utilize My Menu**: Customize the **My Menu** tab with frequently used settings to save time during shoots.
- **Practice**: Regularly use the menu system to become comfortable with accessing and changing settings quickly, especially in fast-paced shooting environments.

Navigating the menu system of the Canon EOS R7 is designed to be intuitive and straightforward, enhancing your shooting experience. By familiarizing yourself with the layout and practice using the settings, you'll be able to efficiently adjust your camera to suit your creative vision, ensuring you never miss a moment.

CHAPTER THREE
CANON EOS R7'S IMAGING SYSTEM

APS-C Sensor and Image Processor

The Canon EOS R7 features a 32.5-megapixel APS-C sensor and an advanced image processor, contributing significantly to its performance in photography and videography. Here's an overview of these key components:

1. APS-C Sensor

- **Size and Format**:
  - The APS-C sensor in the EOS R7 measures approximately 22.3mm x 14.9mm, providing a crop factor of 1.6x compared to full-frame sensors. This size allows for a balance between image quality and portability.

- **High Resolution**:
  - With a resolution of 32.5 megapixels, the sensor captures high levels of detail, making it suitable for a variety of photography styles, including landscapes, portraits, and wildlife. The increased pixel count allows for larger prints and detailed cropping without significant loss of quality.

- **Dynamic Range**:
  - The sensor delivers an impressive dynamic range, enabling it to capture a wider range of tones from shadows to highlights. This is particularly beneficial in challenging lighting conditions, helping to preserve details in both dark and bright areas of an image.

- **Low-Light Performance**:
  - The APS-C sensor provides improved low-light performance, allowing for better image quality at higher ISO settings. This makes the EOS R7 suitable for shooting in dimly lit environments without excessive noise.

- **Dual Pixel CMOS AF II**:
  - The sensor incorporates Canon's Dual Pixel CMOS AF II technology, which provides fast and accurate autofocus across a wide area of the frame. This system allows for smooth and precise focusing in various shooting conditions, enhancing the overall shooting experience.

2. Image Processor

- **DIGIC X Image Processor**:
  - The Canon EOS R7 is powered by the DIGIC X image processor, which enhances overall camera performance, image quality, and speed. The DIGIC X

processor enables faster processing of images and video, resulting in improved responsiveness.

- **Improved Noise Reduction**:
  - The image processor works in tandem with the sensor to reduce noise levels in images, especially at higher ISO settings. This results in cleaner images with more accurate colours, even in challenging lighting situations.

- **Enhanced Autofocus Capabilities**:
  - With the DIGIC X processor, the camera benefits from advanced autofocus capabilities, including Eye Detection AF and Animal Detection AF. These features are crucial for capturing sharp images of moving subjects, such as wildlife or athletes.

- **High-Speed Continuous Shooting**:
  - The combination of the APS-C sensor and DIGIC X processor allows for high-speed continuous shooting of up to 30 frames per second (fps) with the electronic shutter. This feature is particularly useful for action photography, ensuring you capture the perfect moment in fast-paced scenarios.

- **Video Performance**:
  - The image processor also supports high-quality video recording, enabling 4K video at up to 60 fps. This allows for cinematic-quality footage with excellent detail and smooth motion.

The APS-C sensor and DIGIC X image processor in the Canon EOS R7 work together to deliver exceptional image quality, fast autofocus, and impressive low-light performance. These features make the R7 a versatile camera, suitable for a wide range of photography and videography applications, from everyday shooting to more specialized tasks like wildlife and sports photography. By leveraging the strengths of both the sensor and processor, the EOS R7 ensures that photographers can capture stunning images with remarkable clarity and detail.

Dual Pixel Autofocus Technology

Dual Pixel Autofocus (DPAF) is a revolutionary autofocus system introduced by Canon, and it plays a crucial role in the performance of the Canon EOS R7. Here's a detailed look at how this technology works and its advantages:

1. How Dual Pixel Autofocus Works

- **Sensor Design**:
  - Unlike traditional autofocus systems that use phase detection or contrast detection, DPAF utilizes the entire image sensor for focusing. Each pixel on the sensor is split into two photodiodes, allowing for phase detection and providing precise depth information.

- **Phase Detection**:
    - During autofocus, the camera analyses the two signals from each pixel to determine the direction and distance to the subject. This allows for fast and accurate focusing, as the system can quickly gauge whether the subject is in front of or behind the desired focus point.

- **Real-Time Focusing**:
    - DPAF works in real-time while shooting, providing continuous autofocus even when recording video or during live view. This is particularly beneficial for capturing moving subjects, as the camera can track and adjust focus seamlessly.

2. Key Features of Dual Pixel Autofocus in the EOS R7

- **Wide Autofocus Coverage**:
    - The EOS R7 features an extensive autofocus area, covering approximately 100% of the frame. This allows for greater flexibility in composition, as you can place subjects anywhere in the frame without worrying about focus accuracy.

- **High Number of AF Points**:
    - With up to 651 AF points, the EOS R7 provides a dense array of focusing points, allowing for precise focus on subjects, even in complex scenes. The abundance of points enhances tracking capabilities for fast-moving subjects.

- **Eye Detection AF**:
    - The DPAF system includes advanced features like Eye Detection AF, which can automatically detect and focus on a subject's eyes. This is especially useful for portrait photography, ensuring that the eyes are sharp and in focus.

- **Animal Detection AF**:
    - The camera can also recognize and track animals' faces and eyes, making it a valuable tool for wildlife photographers. This feature improves the chances of capturing sharp images of animals in motion.

- **Face Detection**:
    - DPAF enables the camera to recognize faces in a scene, allowing for quick focus adjustment when photographing people. This feature is particularly useful for events, weddings, and candid shots.

3. Advantages of Dual Pixel Autofocus

- **Speed**:
    - The DPAF system is known for its quick focusing capabilities, allowing photographers to capture fleeting moments without lag. The fast response time is crucial for action and sports photography.

- **Accuracy**:
    - DPAF provides accurate focusing, even in low-light situations. The system can effectively lock onto subjects in dim lighting, ensuring that important details are not lost.

- **Smooth Transition**:
    - When shifting focus between subjects, DPAF offers smooth transitions without the "hunting" effect often seen in traditional autofocus systems. This results in more professional-looking videos and stills.

- **Versatility**:
    - The combination of DPAF with the EOS R7's advanced features makes it suitable for various shooting scenarios, from portrait and event photography to wildlife and sports.

The Dual Pixel Autofocus technology in the Canon EOS R7 significantly enhances its performance, providing fast, accurate, and versatile focusing capabilities. Whether you are shooting still images or video, DPAF ensures that your subjects remain sharp and in focus, allowing you to concentrate on creativity rather than technical challenges. This technology is a key feature that sets the EOS R7 apart as a powerful tool for both amateur and professional photographers.

Image Quality and Resolution

The Canon EOS R7 is designed to deliver exceptional image quality and high resolution, making it an ideal choice for photographers and videographers alike. Here's a comprehensive overview of the camera's capabilities in terms of image quality and resolution.

1. High Resolution

- **32.5 Megapixel APS-C Sensor**:
    - The EOS R7 features a 32.5-megapixel APS-C sensor, which provides a high level of detail in images. This resolution is particularly advantageous for photographers who require large prints or want to crop images without sacrificing quality.

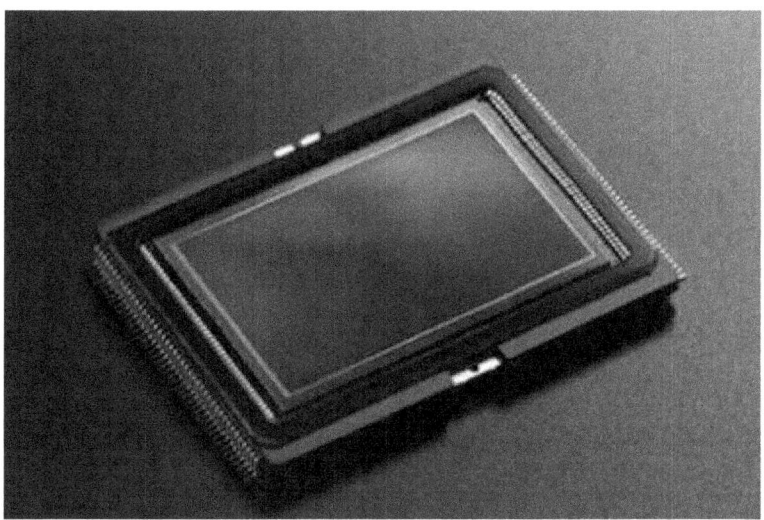

- **Crop Factor**:
    - With its APS-C sensor, the R7 has a crop factor of 1.6x compared to full-frame sensors. This allows photographers to achieve greater effective focal lengths with RF and EF lenses, making it a popular choice for wildlife and sports photography.

2. Image Quality

- **Dynamic Range**:
    - The EOS R7 offers an impressive dynamic range, enabling the camera to capture details in both shadows and highlights. This feature is essential for maintaining image quality in challenging lighting conditions, such as bright sunlight or backlit scenes.

- **Low-Light Performance**:
    - The combination of the sensor design and advanced noise reduction technology ensures that the EOS R7 performs well in low-light situations. Photographers can shoot at higher ISO settings (up to ISO 32,000, expandable to 51,200) while maintaining acceptable noise levels, resulting in cleaner images.

- **Colour Reproduction**:
    - Canon is known for its accurate and vibrant colon reproduction, and the EOS R7 continues this tradition. The camera captures natural skin tones and a broad spectrum of colours, making it suitable for portrait, landscape, and product photography.

- **JPEG and RAW Formats**:
    - The R7 offers the option to shoot in both JPEG and RAW formats. RAW files provide greater flexibility in post-processing, allowing photographers to adjust exposure, white balance, and other settings without degrading image quality.

3. Image Processing

- **DIGIC X Image Processor**:
    - The Canon EOS R7 is equipped with the DIGIC X image processor, which enhances image quality through advanced processing algorithms. This processor improves noise reduction, colour accuracy, and overall image fidelity, ensuring high-quality results in various shooting conditions.

- **High-Speed Continuous Shooting**:
    - The combination of the high-resolution sensor and DIGIC X processor allows for continuous shooting at up to 30 frames per second (fps) with the electronic shutter. This is particularly useful for capturing fast-moving subjects while maintaining high image quality.

4. Video Quality

- **4K Video Recording**:
    - The EOS R7 supports 4K video recording at up to 60 frames per second. This allows for high-resolution video with excellent detail, making it ideal for both amateur and professional videographers. The camera also features 10-bit 4:2:2 internal recording, which enhances colour depth and post-production flexibility.

- **Dual Pixel CMOS AF**:
    - The camera's autofocus system is crucial for maintaining sharp focus during video recording. The Dual Pixel CMOS AF technology ensures smooth and accurate focus transitions, making it easier to capture dynamic scenes.

The Canon EOS R7 excels in image quality and resolution, making it a versatile tool for photographers and videographers. With its high-resolution APS-C sensor, impressive dynamic range, low-light performance, and advanced image processing capabilities, the R7 delivers stunning images that meet the demands of both casual shooters and professionals.

Whether you're capturing breathtaking landscapes, detailed portraits, or high-energy action shots, the EOS R7 is designed to produce exceptional results in a wide range of shooting scenarios.

ISO Sensitivity Range

The Canon EOS R7 features a versatile ISO sensitivity range that enhances its performance in various lighting conditions. Here's an overview of its ISO capabilities:

1. ISO Sensitivity Range

- **Standard Range**:
    - The EOS R7 has a standard ISO sensitivity range of **100 to 32,000**. This allows photographers to capture images in bright conditions without overexposing the highlights.

- **Expanded Range**:
    - For situations requiring even greater sensitivity, the ISO can be expanded to a maximum of **51,200**. This expanded range enables shooting in very low-light environments, making it ideal for indoor photography, nighttime scenes, and astrophotography.

2. Performance at Different ISO Levels

- **Low ISO (100-800)**:
    - At lower ISO settings, the R7 delivers excellent image quality with minimal noise. This range is ideal for landscape photography, studio work, and other well-lit conditions where detail and colour accuracy are paramount.

- **Mid ISO (800-3200)**:
    - The mid-range ISO settings provide good balance between sensitivity and image quality. Photographers can expect clean images with slight noise that is often manageable in post-processing. This range is suitable for events, portraits, and street photography in moderate lighting.

- **High ISO (3200-32,000)**:
    - As ISO levels increase, the R7 maintains decent performance. Noise becomes more noticeable, but the advanced DIGIC X processor and sensor technology help reduce noise effectively. This makes it suitable for low-light scenarios, such as indoor events or evening shoots.

- **Maximum ISO (51,200)**:
    - While the maximum ISO setting provides the ability to shoot in extremely low-light situations, users should be aware that noise can be more pronounced at this level. However, the camera still manages to produce usable images with acceptable quality, especially when processed with noise reduction techniques.

3. Auto ISO Functionality

- The Canon EOS R7 also offers an **Auto ISO** feature, which automatically adjusts the ISO setting based on the lighting conditions and shutter speed. This is particularly useful for photographers who need to capture spontaneous moments without manual adjustments.

- Users can customize Auto ISO settings, including the minimum and maximum ISO levels and the minimum shutter speed, to suit their shooting preferences.

4. Practical Applications

- **Low-Light Photography**: The high ISO capabilities make the R7 a great option for shooting in low-light environments, such as concerts, indoor events, and nighttime scenes.

- **Fast Action Shots**: Higher ISO settings enable faster shutter speeds, allowing for the capture of moving subjects without motion blur, which is beneficial in sports or wildlife photography.

- **Versatility**: The broad ISO range enhances the camera's versatility, enabling photographers to adapt to a variety of lighting situations without the need for additional equipment like external flashes.

The ISO sensitivity range of the Canon EOS R7, from 100 to 32,000 (expandable to 51,200), provides photographers with flexibility and versatility for shooting in diverse lighting conditions. Its ability to maintain image quality at high ISO settings, combined with advanced noise reduction technology, makes the R7 a powerful tool for capturing stunning images in both bright and low-light environments.

Whether you're shooting landscapes during golden hour or capturing candid moments at night, the EOS R7 is equipped to deliver impressive results.

CHAPTER FOUR
LENS AND ACCCESSORIES

Compatible RF and EF Lenses

The Canon EOS R7 is compatible with both RF and EF lenses, providing photographers with a wide range of options to suit their specific needs and shooting styles. Here's a detailed overview of the lens compatibility:

1. RF Lenses

RF lenses are specifically designed for Canon's mirrorless cameras, offering advanced optical performance and features tailored for the EOS R system. Some notable RF lenses compatible with the EOS R7 include:

- **RF 24-105mm f/4L IS USM**:
    - A versatile standard zoom lens that covers a popular focal length range, ideal for various photography genres, including landscapes, portraits, and events.

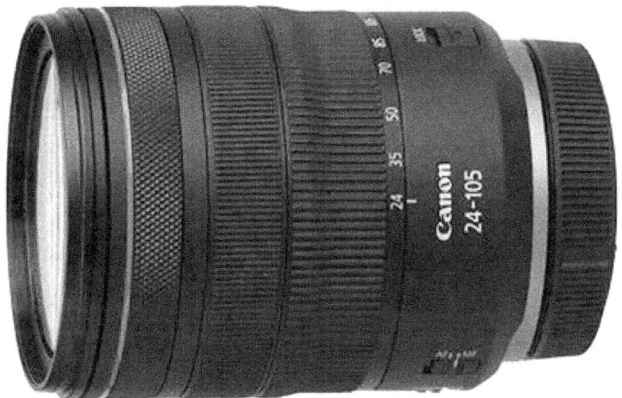

- **RF 15-35mm f/2.8L IS USM**:
    - This ultra-wide-angle zoom lens is perfect for landscape, architecture, and interior photography, with a fast maximum aperture for low-light performance.

- **RF 50mm f/1.2L USM**:
    - A fast prime lens that excels in portrait photography, providing stunning bokeh and excellent low-light capabilities.

- **RF 85mm f/1.2L USM**:
    - An excellent choice for portrait photographers, this lens offers beautiful background separation and sharpness at wide apertures.

- **RF 100-500mm f/4.5-7.1L IS USM**:
    - A versatile telephoto zoom lens suitable for wildlife and sports photography, providing a wide focal range for capturing distant subjects.

2. EF Lenses

EF lenses, designed for Canon's DSLR cameras, can be used with the EOS R7 through the **EF-EOS R Mount Adapter**. This adapter allows full compatibility, preserving autofocus and image stabilization features. Some popular EF lenses include:

- **EF 24-70mm f/2.8L II USM**:
  - A professional-grade standard zoom lens, excellent for portraiture, weddings, and general photography.

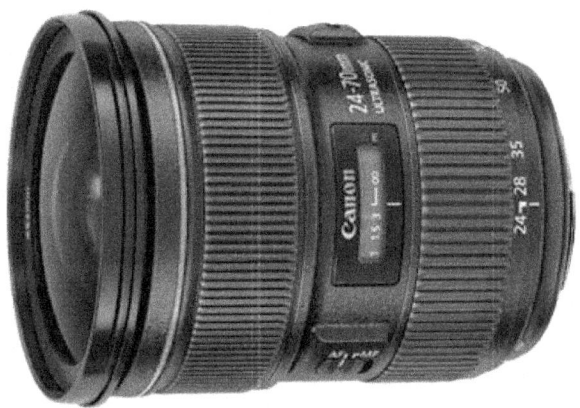

- **EF 70-200mm f/2.8L IS III USM**:
  - A favourite among sports and wildlife photographers, this telephoto lens offers exceptional image quality and fast autofocus.

- **EF 50mm f/1.8 STM**:
  - A compact and affordable prime lens that delivers impressive sharpness and beautiful bokeh, perfect for portraits and low-light situations.

- **EF 16-35mm f/4L IS USM**:
  - A wide-angle zoom lens that's great for landscape and architecture photography, providing sharpness and versatility.

- **EF 100mm f/2.8L Macro IS USM**:
  - Ideal for macro photography, this lens provides excellent detail and image stabilization for close-up shots.

3. Lens Adapter Options

- **EF-EOS R Mount Adapter**:
  - This adapter allows for seamless use of EF and EF-S lenses on the EOS R7, maintaining autofocus and image stabilization capabilities. There are also versions of the adapter with additional features like a control ring for customizable settings.

- **Control Ring Mount Adapter**:
    - This version of the adapter includes a customizable control ring, allowing users to adjust settings like aperture, ISO, or exposure compensation directly on the adapter, enhancing workflow efficiency.

The Canon EOS R7 offers extensive compatibility with both RF and EF lenses, making it a versatile choice for photographers across various genres. Whether you prefer the advanced optics of RF lenses or the established performance of EF lenses, the R7 provides the flexibility to achieve your creative vision.

The availability of lens adapters further expands your options, allowing you to leverage Canon's rich lens ecosystem while enjoying the benefits of a mirrorless system.

Adapters for EF Lenses

The Canon EOS R7 can utilize EF and EF-S lenses through the use of adapters, allowing photographers to take advantage of Canon's extensive lens lineup. Here's an overview of the available adapters and their features:

1. EF-EOS R Mount Adapter

- **Standard EF-EOS R Adapter**:
    - This is the basic adapter that allows EF and EF-S lenses to be mounted on the EOS R7. It provides seamless integration, enabling the use of autofocus and image stabilization features.

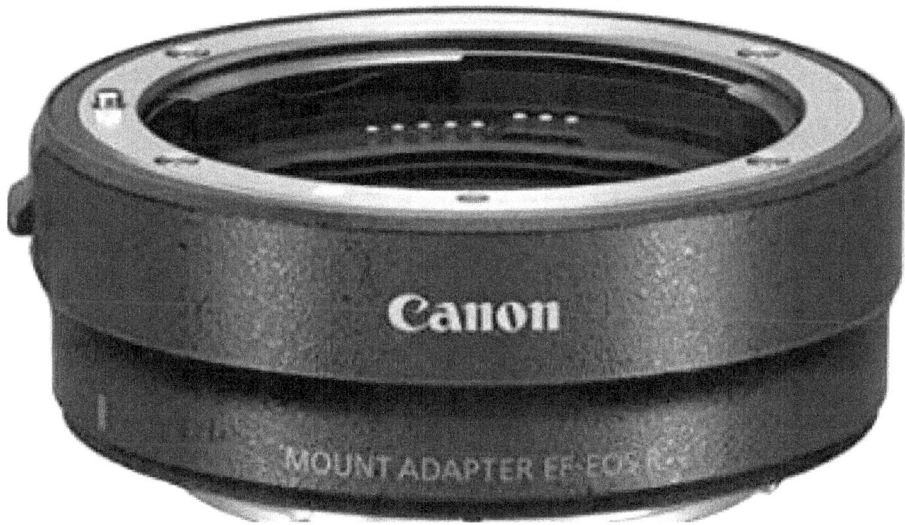

- **Key Features**:
    - Maintains full electronic communication between the camera and lens, ensuring accurate autofocus and aperture control.
    - Supports image stabilization, allowing for smoother handheld shooting.
    - Compact design, preserving the lightweight benefits of the mirrorless system.

2. Control Ring Mount Adapter

- **Control Ring EF-EOS R Adapter**:
    - This version of the adapter includes a customizable control ring that can be assigned to various functions such as aperture, ISO, or exposure compensation.
- **Key Features**:
    - Offers the same benefits as the standard adapter, including autofocus and image stabilization.
    - The additional control ring enhances shooting efficiency, allowing photographers to make quick adjustments without taking their hands off the camera.

3. EF-EOS R Mount Adapter with Drop-in Filter Slot

- **Drop-in Filter Adapter**:
    - This adapter incorporates a drop-in filter slot, enabling the use of filters like circular polarizers or ND filters without needing to attach them directly to the lens.
- **Key Features**:
    - Maintains all functionalities of the standard EF-EOS R adapter.
    - Provides flexibility in filter usage, particularly beneficial for photographers who frequently use filters for landscape or long exposure photography.
    - The drop-in design allows for quick filter changes, making it convenient for on-the-go shooting.

4. Advantages of Using Adapters

- **Versatility**:
    - The ability to use EF and EF-S lenses on the EOS R7 expands your creative options, allowing you to leverage existing lenses or explore the full range of Canon's lens offerings.
- **Cost-Effective**:
    - For photographers transitioning to mirrorless systems, using adapters allows them to keep their investment in EF lenses while adopting the newer EOS R system without needing to buy all new lenses.

- **Maintaining Performance**:
    - Canon's adapters ensure that the performance characteristics of the lenses—such as autofocus speed and image stabilization—are maintained, providing a seamless shooting experience.

The Canon EOS R7 benefits significantly from the availability of EF-EOS R mount adapters, which allow for extensive compatibility with EF and EF-S lenses. Whether you choose the standard adapter, the control ring version, or the drop-in filter adapter, these options enhance the camera's versatility and usability.

By utilizing these adapters, photographers can enjoy the best of both worlds—leveraging the strengths of Canon's established DSLR lens lineup while taking advantage of the advanced features and benefits of the EOS R7 mirrorless system.

Essential Accessories (Batteries, Memory Cards, Grips)

To maximize the performance and versatility of the Canon EOS R7, several essential accessories can enhance your shooting experience. Here's a look at the most important accessories, including batteries, memory cards, and grips:

1. Batteries

- **LP-E6NH Battery**:
    - The Canon EOS R7 uses the LP-E6NH rechargeable lithium-ion battery, which provides extended shooting time and performance.

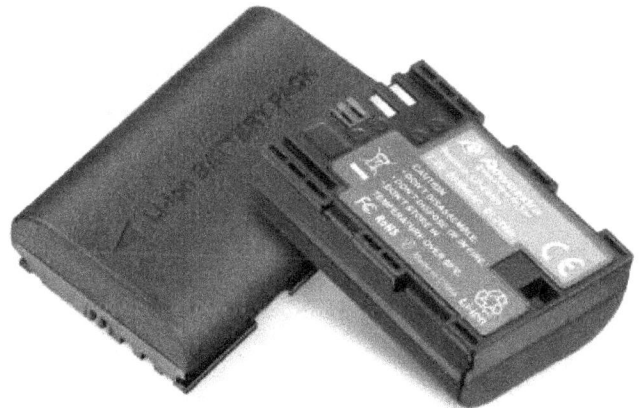

- **Key Features**:
    - **Capacity**: The LP-E6NH offers improved capacity compared to its predecessor (LP-E6N), allowing for approximately **1,000 shots** on a full charge (CIPA standard).
    - **Compatibility**: It is also compatible with previous models that use the LP-E6 battery, making it a versatile option for photographers with other Canon cameras.

- o **Battery Grip**: Consider the **BG-R10 Battery Grip**, which can hold two LP-E6NH batteries for even longer shooting times and improved ergonomics.

2. Memory Cards

- **CFexpress Type B and SD UHS-II Cards**:
  - o The EOS R7 features dual card slots, accommodating both **CFexpress Type B** and **SD UHS-II** memory cards. This allows for high-speed data transfer, ideal for capturing high-resolution images and 4K video.
- **Recommended Cards**:
  - o **CFexpress Type B**:
    - Cards such as the **SanDisk Extreme PRO CFexpress 2.0** or the **Lexar Professional CFexpress Type B** are excellent choices, offering high read/write speeds necessary for continuous shooting and 4K video recording.
  - o **SD UHS-II**:
    - For the SD card slot, consider cards like the **Lexar Professional 2000x** or **SanDisk Extreme PRO SD UHS-II**, which provide fast speeds for quick data writing and reliable performance.

3. Camera Grips

- **BG-R10 Battery Grip**:
  - o This optional battery grip is designed for the EOS R7, enhancing ergonomics and providing additional functionality.

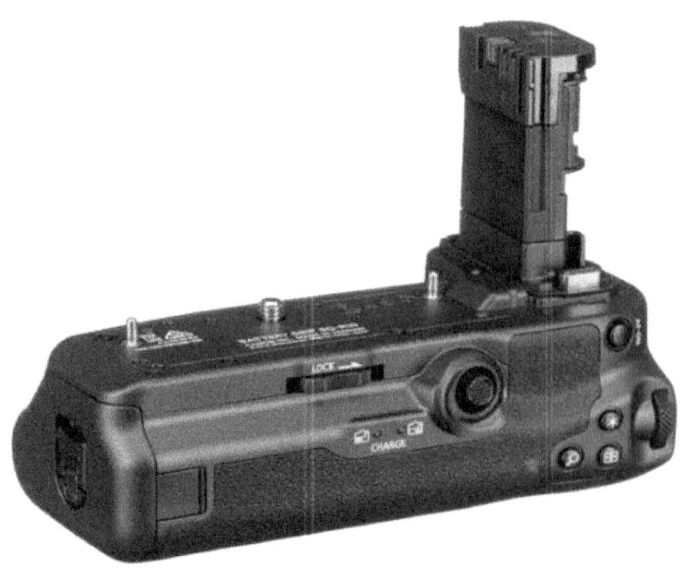

- **Key Features**:
  - **Dual Battery Capacity**: Holds two LP-E6NH batteries, effectively doubling your shooting time, making it ideal for long shoots or events.
  - **Vertical Shooting Controls**: Includes additional controls for portrait orientation shooting, such as a shutter button, control dials, and customizable buttons, making it easier to operate the camera in vertical mode.
  - **Durability**: The grip adds stability, especially when using larger lenses, improving overall handling and comfort during extended shooting sessions.

4. Other Essential Accessories

- **Camera Bag**:
  - A quality camera bag helps protect your gear during transport. Look for a bag with customizable compartments to fit your camera, lenses, and accessories.

- **Tripod**:
  - A sturdy tripod is essential for landscape, long-exposure, and low-light photography. Consider tripods with adjustable height and stability for versatile shooting options.

- **Filters**:
  - Circular polarizers and ND filters can enhance your photography by controlling reflections and managing exposure in bright conditions.

- **Screen Protector**:
  - A screen protector can safeguard the LCD from scratches and damage, ensuring that your display remains in top condition.

- **Cleaning Kit**:
  - A basic cleaning kit, including lens cleaning solution, microfiber cloths, and a blower, helps maintain your equipment and ensures clear images.

Equipping your Canon EOS R7 with essential accessories such as batteries, memory cards, camera grips, and additional gear can significantly enhance your shooting experience. These accessories improve battery life, storage capacity, handling, and overall performance, allowing you to capture stunning images and videos without interruption.

Whether you're a professional photographer or an enthusiast, investing in these accessories will ensure you get the most out of your EOS R7.

CHAPTER FIVE
MASTERING CAMERA MODES

Auto Mode and Scene Modes

The Canon EOS R7 offers various shooting modes that cater to photographers of all skill levels. Among these modes, Auto Mode and Scene Modes provide convenient options for capturing great images without extensive knowledge of camera settings. Here's an overview of these modes:

1. Auto Mode

- **Overview**:
  - Auto Mode is designed for beginners and casual photographers who want to take photos quickly and easily. In this mode, the camera automatically selects the optimal settings for various shooting conditions.

- **Key Features**:
  - **Full Automatic Operation**: The camera handles exposure (shutter speed, aperture, and ISO), white balance, and focus, allowing users to concentrate solely on composition.
  - **Smart Auto Detection**: The EOS R7 analyses the scene and makes intelligent decisions to optimize image quality, making it suitable for a wide range of situations.
  - **Focus Modes**: The camera uses its Dual Pixel autofocus system to ensure fast and accurate focusing, even in challenging conditions.
  - **User-Friendly Interface**: The simple interface makes it easy for novice users to start shooting without adjusting complex settings.

- **When to Use**:
  - Auto Mode is perfect for everyday photography, family events, and travel when you want to capture moments quickly without adjusting settings.

2. Scene Modes

Scene Modes allow users to optimize their camera settings for specific types of photography. The EOS R7 includes various preset modes tailored for different scenarios, enabling users to achieve the best results. Here are some of the key Scene Modes available:

- **Portrait**:
  - Optimizes settings for capturing flattering skin tones and smooth backgrounds. Ideal for portraits and close-up shots.

- **Landscape**:

- o Adjusts settings to enhance depth of field and sharpness, perfect for scenic views and wide landscapes.
- **Close-Up (Macro)**:
  - o Optimizes focus and exposure for capturing detailed close-up images of subjects like flowers or small objects.
- **Sports**:
  - o Increases shutter speed and optimizes autofocus for fast-moving subjects, making it suitable for action shots and sports photography.
- **Night Portrait**:
  - o Combines flash with a longer exposure to capture subjects in low light while maintaining background details. Ideal for evening events.
- **Night Scene**:
  - o Optimizes settings for capturing nighttime landscapes without flash, ensuring good exposure and detail.
- **Food**:
  - o Adjusts colours and tones to enhance food photography, making dishes look more appetizing.
- **Sunset**:
  - o Enhances colours and contrast for capturing the vibrant hues of sunsets.

3. Using Auto and Scene Modes

- **Switching Modes**:
  - o Users can easily switch between Auto and Scene Modes using the mode dial on the camera. Simply turn the dial to the desired mode and start shooting.
- **Creative Flexibility**:
  - o While Auto and Scene Modes are automatic, they also allow for some creative flexibility. Users can adjust settings like exposure compensation to influence the final image without switching to manual controls.

The Auto Mode and Scene Modes on the Canon EOS R7 provide an excellent starting point for novice photographers and a quick solution for experienced shooters in various situations. Auto Mode simplifies the shooting process by handling all settings, while Scene Modes optimize settings for specific types of photography.

These features make the EOS R7 a versatile and user-friendly camera, allowing users to capture stunning images with ease, regardless of their skill level.

Manual Mode (M)

Manual Mode (M) on the Canon EOS R7 gives photographers complete control over their camera settings, allowing for a tailored shooting experience. This mode is ideal for those who want to creatively control exposure, depth of field, and motion blur. Here's a detailed overview of Manual Mode:

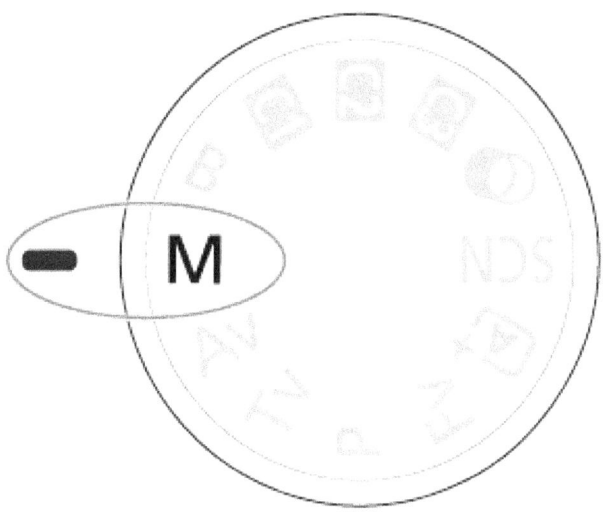

1. Overview of Manual Mode (M)

- **Complete Control**:
    - In Manual Mode, the photographer sets the **shutter speed**, **aperture**, and **ISO** independently. This allows for precise control over the exposure and the ability to adapt to various lighting conditions.

- **Creativity and Flexibility**:
    - Manual Mode is perfect for creative photography, enabling users to experiment with different settings to achieve desired effects, such as long exposures, shallow depth of field, or high dynamic range.

2. Key Settings in Manual Mode

- **Shutter Speed**:
    - Determines how long the camera's sensor is exposed to light. Faster shutter speeds freeze motion, while slower speeds can create motion blur for artistic effects. Users can select speeds from 1/4000s to 30 seconds, depending on the situation.

- **Aperture**:
    - Controls the size of the lens opening, affecting depth of field and the amount of light entering the camera. A wide aperture (low f-stop number) creates a shallow depth of field, ideal for portraits, while a narrow aperture (high f-stop number) increases depth of field, suitable for landscapes.

- **ISO**:
    - Adjusts the camera's sensitivity to light. Lower ISO values (e.g., 100 or 200) produce cleaner images with less noise in well-lit conditions, while higher ISO values (e.g., 1600 or higher) can be used in low-light situations but may introduce noise.

3. Exposure Metering

- The EOS R7 features an **exposure meter** that helps photographers gauge the exposure level. The meter displays in the viewfinder or on the LCD screen, indicating whether the current settings will produce an underexposed, correctly exposed, or overexposed image.
- Users can adjust the shutter speed, aperture, and ISO until the meter indicates proper exposure, often represented by a central marker in the viewfinder.

4. Benefits of Using Manual Mode

- **Full Creative Control**:
    - Photographers can experiment with settings to create unique images and achieve specific artistic goals, such as capturing motion blur or achieving a dreamy background effect.
- **Adaptation to Challenging Lighting**:
    - In situations with mixed lighting or rapidly changing conditions, Manual Mode allows users to quickly adapt their settings for the best exposure.
- **Learning Opportunity**:
    - Using Manual Mode encourages photographers to learn about exposure triangle (shutter speed, aperture, ISO) and how each setting affects the final image. This knowledge is crucial for improving photography skills.

5. Using Manual Mode Effectively

- **Practice**:
    - Regular practice in Manual Mode helps build familiarity with how each setting influences exposure and image quality.
- **Histogram**:
    - Utilizing the histogram feature can aid in evaluating exposure. A well-balanced histogram should be cantered, avoiding clipping on either side, indicating loss of highlight or shadow detail.

- **Bracketing**:
    - Consider using exposure bracketing to capture multiple exposures of the same scene. This technique is useful for HDR photography, where you can combine images with different exposures to achieve a balanced final result.

Manual Mode (M) on the Canon EOS R7 is an invaluable tool for photographers seeking to take full control of their creative process. By independently adjusting shutter speed, aperture, and ISO, users can tailor their settings to suit specific shooting scenarios and achieve their desired artistic vision.

While it may take time to master, the skills gained through practicing in Manual Mode will significantly enhance a photographer's abilities and confidence.

Aperture Priority (Av)

Aperture Priority Mode (Av) is a popular shooting mode on the Canon EOS R7 that allows photographers to control the aperture setting while the camera automatically adjusts the shutter speed for optimal exposure. This mode is especially useful for those who want to manage depth of field while still maintaining control over exposure. Here's a comprehensive overview of Aperture Priority Mode:

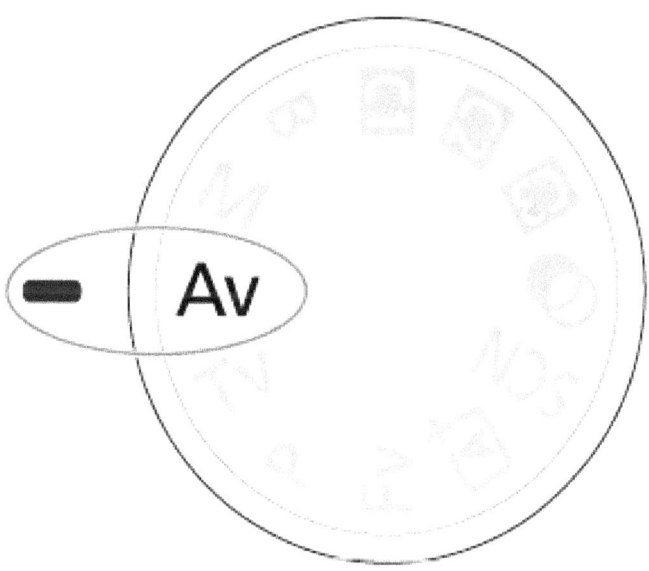

1. Overview of Aperture Priority Mode (Av)

- **Control Over Aperture**:
    - In Av Mode, you set the aperture (f-stop), which determines the size of the lens opening. This allows you to influence the depth of field, or how much of the image is in focus, while the camera takes care of the shutter speed.

- **Automatic Exposure**:
    - The camera calculates the appropriate shutter speed based on the chosen aperture and the current lighting conditions, ensuring that the image is properly exposed.

2. Key Features

- **Depth of Field Control**:
  - Aperture Priority Mode is ideal for creative control over depth of field.
  - **Wide Apertures (Low f-stop)**: Creating a shallow depth of field, which is perfect for portraits where you want the subject to stand out against a blurred background.
  - **Narrow Apertures (High f-stop)**: Increasing the depth of field, making it suitable for landscape photography where you want everything in focus from foreground to background.

- **Exposure Compensation**:
  - You can use exposure compensation in Av Mode to adjust the exposure level. This is useful if you want to deliberately overexpose or underexpose the image, such as in high-contrast lighting situations.

3. Using Aperture Priority Mode Effectively

- **Setting the Aperture**:
  - To use Av Mode, turn the mode dial to "Av" and then adjust the aperture using the main dial on the camera. The selected f-stop will be displayed in the viewfinder or on the LCD screen.

- **Monitoring Shutter Speed**:
  - While in Av Mode, keep an eye on the shutter speed displayed in the viewfinder. If the shutter speed drops too low (potentially causing motion blur), consider adjusting the aperture to a wider setting or increasing the ISO for better light sensitivity.

- **Consider Lighting Conditions**:
  - In low-light situations, using a wider aperture can help maintain a faster shutter speed. Conversely, in bright conditions, you may need to use a narrower aperture or reduce ISO to prevent overexposure.

4. When to Use Aperture Priority Mode (Av)

- **Portrait Photography**:
  - Use Av Mode to set a wide aperture for beautiful bokeh and soft backgrounds, ensuring the subject stands out.

- **Landscape Photography**:
  - Choose a narrow aperture to achieve maximum sharpness throughout the image, capturing all details from foreground to background.

- **Creative Effects**:
  - Use the mode for artistic effects, such as selective focus or when shooting subjects in motion against a blurred background.

5. Benefits of Using Aperture Priority Mode

- **Simplified Exposure Management**:
  - By focusing on the aperture, photographers can quickly adapt to different scenes while leaving the shutter speed adjustment to the camera.

- **Ideal for Fast-Paced Shooting**:
  - Av Mode is particularly useful in dynamic environments where lighting conditions change quickly, such as during events or nature photography.

- **Learning Opportunity**:
  - This mode provides an excellent opportunity for photographers to understand the relationship between aperture, depth of field, and exposure, enhancing their overall photography skills.

Aperture Priority Mode (Av) on the Canon EOS R7 is a powerful tool for photographers looking to exert creative control over depth of field while allowing the camera to manage exposure automatically.

By mastering this mode, photographers can enhance their ability to capture stunning images in a variety of conditions, making it a favourite choice for both enthusiasts and professionals alike.

Shutter Priority (Tv)

Shutter Priority Mode (Tv) on the Canon EOS R7 allows photographers to take control of the shutter speed while the camera automatically adjusts the aperture to ensure proper exposure. This mode is particularly useful for capturing fast-moving subjects or creating motion blur effects. Here's an in-depth overview of Shutter Priority Mode:

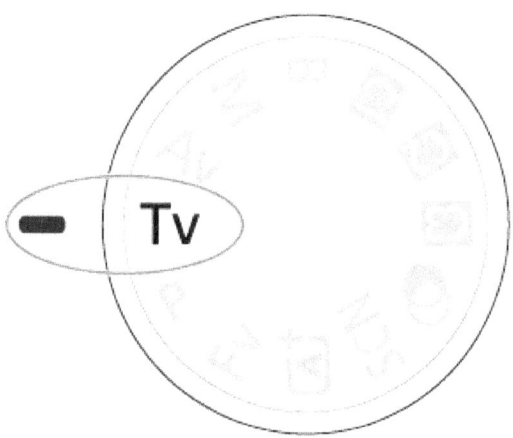

1. Overview of Shutter Priority Mode (Tv)

- **Control Over Shutter Speed**:
    - In Tv Mode, you set the shutter speed, which determines how long the camera's sensor is exposed to light. The camera calculates the necessary aperture to achieve the correct exposure based on the selected shutter speed.

- **Automatic Exposure**:
    - The camera automatically adjusts the aperture to ensure that the image is properly exposed, making it easier to focus on motion and timing.

2. Key Features

- **Motion Control**:
    - Shutter Priority Mode is ideal for managing motion in your photography.
    - **Fast Shutter Speeds**: Useful for freezing action in sports or wildlife photography. For example, a shutter speed of 1/1000s or faster can effectively freeze a moving subject.
    - **Slow Shutter Speeds**: Suitable for creating motion blur effects, such as the smooth flow of water in a waterfall or the movement of cars in light trails.

- **Exposure Compensation**:
    - Like Aperture Priority Mode, Tv Mode allows for exposure compensation. This is beneficial in situations where the camera's metering might misinterpret the scene, such as high-contrast or backlit situations.

3. Using Shutter Priority Mode Effectively

- **Setting the Shutter Speed**:
    - To engage Tv Mode, turn the mode dial to "Tv" and adjust the shutter speed using the main dial. The selected speed will be displayed in the viewfinder or on the LCD screen.

- **Monitoring Aperture**:
    - Keep an eye on the aperture value displayed in the viewfinder. If the aperture reaches its maximum or minimum limit (i.e., f-stop is too low or high), the camera may not be able to achieve the desired exposure.

- **Consider Lighting Conditions**:
    - In low-light situations, using a slower shutter speed can help capture enough light but may introduce motion blur if the subject is moving. In bright conditions, you may need to use a faster shutter speed to avoid overexposure.

4. When to Use Shutter Priority Mode (Tv)

- **Sports Photography**:
    - Use Tv Mode to set a fast shutter speed to capture sharp images of athletes in motion, ensuring that action is frozen without blur.

- **Wildlife Photography**:
    - Ideal for photographing animals, where quick movements are common. Setting a fast shutter speed ensures that fleeting moments are captured in detail.

- **Creative Motion Effects**:
    - Use slower shutter speeds to capture creative motion effects, such as light trails or the blur of moving subjects, adding a dynamic element to your images.

5. Benefits of Using Shutter Priority Mode

- **Quick Adaptation**:
    - Tv Mode allows photographers to quickly adapt to changing conditions by focusing on shutter speed while leaving aperture adjustments to the camera.

- **Ideal for Fast-Paced Shooting**:
    - This mode is especially useful in dynamic environments, such as sporting events or street photography, where rapid changes in motion occur.

- **Learning Opportunity**:
    - Using Shutter Priority Mode helps photographers understand the relationship between shutter speed, motion, and exposure, enhancing overall photography skills.

Shutter Priority Mode (Tv) on the Canon EOS R7 empowers photographers to capture fast-moving subjects and create unique motion effects by prioritizing shutter speed control. By mastering this mode, photographers can enhance their ability to adapt to different shooting scenarios, ensuring that they achieve the desired results, whether they are freezing action or exploring creative blur effects.

Program Mode (P)

Program Mode (P) on the Canon EOS R7 offers a balanced approach to photography by automatically setting both shutter speed and aperture while allowing users to make adjustments to exposure settings. This mode is great for those who want the convenience of automatic exposure with the flexibility to control certain parameters.

Here's a detailed overview of Program Mode:

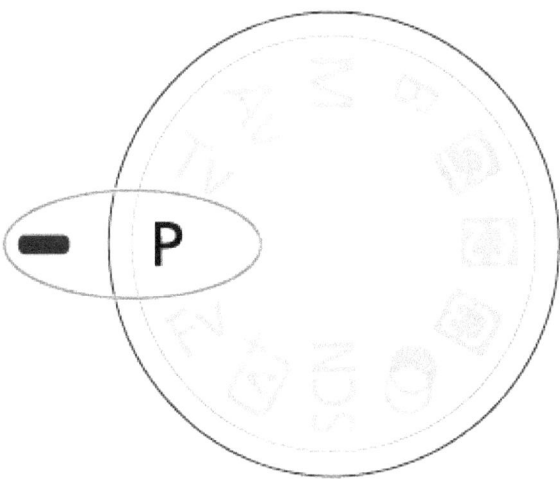

1. Overview of Program Mode (P)

- **Automatic Exposure Control**:
    - In Program Mode, the camera automatically selects an appropriate shutter speed and aperture combination for the current lighting conditions, ensuring a well-exposed image.

- **Flexible Adjustments**:
    - While the camera sets the basic exposure parameters, photographers can adjust the exposure compensation, ISO, and other settings, allowing for some creative control over the image.

2. Key Features

- **Intelligent Exposure**:
    - The EOS R7 uses its metering system to evaluate the scene and determine the optimal shutter speed and aperture combination. This is useful in a variety of lighting situations, from bright daylight to dimly lit environments.

- **Program Shift**:
    - One of the unique features of Program Mode is the **Program Shift** function. Users can adjust the combination of shutter speed and aperture after the camera has made its initial selection. This allows for creative adjustments without switching to another shooting mode.

- For example, if the camera selects a fast shutter speed, users can shift to a different aperture while maintaining the same exposure level.

3. Using Program Mode Effectively

- **Setting Up Program Mode**:
    - To activate Program Mode, simply turn the mode dial to "P." The camera will automatically select the shutter speed and aperture for the current scene.

- **Adjusting Settings**:
    - Use the camera controls to adjust ISO and exposure compensation as needed. This is particularly useful in high-contrast situations or when creative effects are desired.

- **Utilizing Program Shift**:
    - If you want to change the depth of field or freeze motion while keeping the exposure consistent, you can use the Program Shift feature to adjust the settings. This is done by turning the main dial to change the aperture or shutter speed.

4. When to Use Program Mode (P)

- **Everyday Photography**:
    - Program Mode is perfect for casual shooting situations, such as family gatherings, travel, or street photography, where you want to capture moments quickly without delving into complex settings.

- **Event Photography**:
    - In dynamic environments where lighting conditions can change rapidly, Program Mode allows for quick adjustments and reliable exposure.

- **Learning Tool**:
    - Program Mode serves as a great learning tool for novice photographers. It provides the opportunity to observe how different shutter speeds and apertures affect exposure while still offering the convenience of automatic settings.

5. Benefits of Using Program Mode

- **Convenience**:
    - Program Mode allows for quick and easy shooting, making it ideal for photographers who want to capture images without worrying about technical settings.

- **Balance of Control and Automation**:
    - This mode provides a nice balance between automatic exposure and manual control, making it suitable for various shooting scenarios.
- **Exploration of Exposure Settings**:
    - The flexibility of Program Shift encourages experimentation with different settings, helping photographers understand the exposure triangle (shutter speed, aperture, ISO) better.

Program Mode (P) on the Canon EOS R7 offers photographers a convenient way to capture images with automatic exposure control while retaining the ability to make creative adjustments.

This mode is particularly useful for everyday shooting, allowing photographers to focus on composition and moments without getting bogged down by technical details. By mastering Program Mode, photographers can enhance their skills and confidence in various shooting environments.

CHAPTER SIX
AUTOFOCUS AND TRACKING SYSTEMS

AF Modes and Functions

The Canon EOS R7 features advanced autofocus (AF) capabilities, making it an excellent choice for capturing sharp images in various shooting scenarios. Understanding the different AF modes and functions is essential for maximizing the camera's performance.

Here's a comprehensive overview of the AF modes and functions available on the Canon EOS R7:

1. Overview of Autofocus (AF) System

The EOS R7 utilizes Canon's Dual Pixel CMOS AF II technology, which offers fast and accurate focusing, ideal for both still photography and video. This system allows for smooth focusing transitions, making it suitable for dynamic subjects.

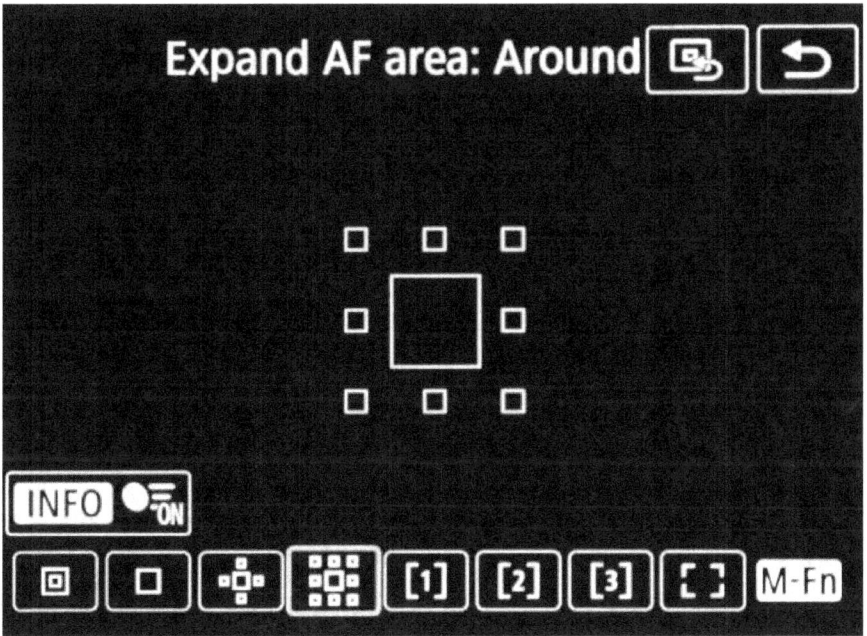

2. AF Modes

The Canon EOS R7 provides several AF modes, each designed for different shooting situations:

- **One-Shot AF (Single AF):**
    - This mode is ideal for stationary subjects. When you half-press the shutter button, the camera focuses on the subject and locks the focus. It is perfect for landscapes, portraits, and other scenes where the subject is not moving.

- **AI Servo AF (Continuous AF):**
    - AI Servo AF is designed for moving subjects. The camera continuously adjusts focus as the subject moves, ensuring that the subject remains sharp. This mode is ideal for sports, wildlife, and action photography.

- **AI Focus AF**:
    - AI Focus AF automatically switches between One-Shot AF and AI Servo AF based on whether the subject is stationary or in motion. This mode is useful in unpredictable shooting environments where the subject's movement may change.

3. AF Points and Area Selection

The EOS R7 features an extensive AF point system, allowing for precise focusing across the frame:

- **Wide Area AF**:
    - This mode allows the camera to use a large number of AF points to achieve focus. It is helpful for capturing subjects that are not centred in the frame.

- **Zone AF**:
    - Zone AF lets you select a specific zone within the frame, making it easier to track subjects in a defined area. This is useful for sports or wildlife photography where the subject moves within a limited space.

- **Spot AF**:
    - Spot AF is the most precise focusing mode, using a small AF point to achieve accurate focus on small or detailed subjects. This is ideal for macro photography or when focusing on specific areas of a subject.

- **Expand AF Area**:
    - This function allows the camera to use surrounding AF points to assist with focus if the main point fails to acquire focus, which is beneficial for tracking moving subjects.

4. AF Functions

In addition to the AF modes, the Canon EOS R7 includes several functions that enhance its autofocus capabilities:

- **Face and Eye Detection**:
    - The EOS R7 features advanced face and eye detection AF, automatically identifying and focusing on human faces and eyes. This is particularly useful for portrait photography, ensuring sharp focus on the subject's eyes.

- **Animal Detection AF**:
    - This feature detects and focuses on animals' faces and eyes, making it ideal for wildlife photographers. The camera can recognize various animal types, allowing for accurate focus on fast-moving subjects.

- **Tracking**:
    - The camera can track subjects across the frame, ensuring consistent focus as they move. This is particularly useful for sports and action photography where subjects can change positions quickly.

- **Subject Tracking Settings**:
    - The EOS R7 allows users to customize tracking sensitivity and speed, making it easier to adapt to different shooting situations. This flexibility is essential for capturing fast-moving subjects effectively.

5. Using AF Modes and Functions Effectively

- **Choosing the Right Mode**:
    - Select One-Shot AF for static subjects, AI Servo for moving subjects, and AI Focus for unpredictable movements. Understanding the environment and the subject's behaviour is crucial for selecting the appropriate AF mode.

- **Utilizing AF Points**:
    - Take advantage of the wide range of AF points and area selection modes. Use Zone AF or Spot AF for more control over focus, particularly when dealing with intricate compositions.

- **Experimenting with Detection Features**:
    - Experiment with face and eye detection, as well as animal detection AF, to see how they improve your photography, especially in portrait and wildlife scenarios.

The autofocus modes and functions of the Canon EOS R7 provide photographers with powerful tools to achieve sharp and accurate focus in various shooting situations. By understanding and utilizing the different AF modes, points, and functions, photographers can enhance their ability to capture compelling images, whether shooting stills or videos. Mastering these features will significantly improve overall shooting experience and outcomes.

Face and Eye Detection

The Canon EOS R7 is equipped with advanced Face and Eye Detection technology, enhancing its autofocus capabilities for portrait and wildlife photography. This feature ensures that the camera accurately focuses on the subject's face and eyes, resulting in sharper and more engaging images.

Here's an in-depth overview of the Face and Eye Detection functionality:

1. Overview of Face and Eye Detection

- **Purpose**:
    - Face and Eye Detection is designed to automatically recognize human faces and eyes within the frame. This technology ensures that the camera focuses precisely on the most important parts of a portrait: the subject's eyes.

- **Automatic Focus Adjustment**:
    - The system continually adjusts focus as the subject moves, ensuring that the eyes remain sharp and in focus, which is crucial for captivating portrait photography.

2. How Face and Eye Detection Works

- **Detection Process**:
    - When you press the shutter button halfway, the camera analyses the scene for faces. Once detected, it locks focus on the nearest face or eye, depending on the selected settings.

- **Eye Detection**:
    - The EOS R7 can specifically target and focus on a subject's eye. If multiple faces are detected, the camera can prioritize which eye to focus on, typically favouring the eye that is closer to the camera.

- **Tracking**:
    - If the subject moves after the initial focus is set, the camera continues to track the face or eye, adjusting the focus dynamically to ensure the subject remains sharp throughout the shot.

3. Using Face and Eye Detection Effectively

- **Activating the Feature**:
    - Face and Eye Detection can be activated through the camera's menu settings. Users can enable it in the AF menu and customize various parameters to suit their shooting preferences.

- **Selecting the Detection Mode**:
    - Photographers can choose between different detection modes:
        - **Face Detection**: Focuses on the face of the subject.
        - **Eye Detection**: Prioritizes focus on the subject's eyes, making it ideal for portraits.
- **Customizing Tracking Settings**:
    - Users can adjust the tracking sensitivity and the speed at which the camera reacts to moving subjects. This customization helps achieve optimal results in varying shooting conditions.

4. Benefits of Face and Eye Detection

- **Enhanced Portrait Quality**:
    - By ensuring that the eyes are in sharp focus, photographers can capture more engaging and compelling portraits, highlighting the subject's expression and personality.
- **Efficiency in Shooting**:
    - The automatic focus adjustment saves time, allowing photographers to concentrate on composition and timing rather than manual focus adjustments.
- **Versatility in Various Scenarios**:
    - The feature is beneficial not only in portrait photography but also in capturing candid moments at events, where subjects may be moving or not posing for the camera.
- **Animal Eye Detection**:
    - The EOS R7 also features Animal Eye Detection, which works similarly to human detection. This is particularly useful for wildlife photography, allowing photographers to focus on animals' eyes for sharp, compelling images.

5. Limitations and Considerations

- **Lighting Conditions**:
    - While the Face and Eye Detection system performs well in various lighting conditions, it may struggle in extremely low light or high-contrast scenarios. In such cases, manual focus or other AF modes may be more effective.

- **Complex Backgrounds**:
  - The system may sometimes focus on elements in the background if they resemble human faces or if there are multiple subjects in the frame. It's essential to monitor the focus point and make adjustments if necessary.

The Face and Eye Detection feature on the Canon EOS R7 significantly enhances the camera's ability to capture stunning portraits and candid moments by ensuring that the subject's eyes are sharp and in focus.

By understanding how to utilize this technology effectively, photographers can improve their portraiture skills, capture meaningful moments, and achieve a higher level of detail and engagement in their images. Whether shooting portraits or wildlife, this feature provides a valuable tool for enhancing the overall photography experience.

Subject Tracking Features

The Canon EOS R7 is equipped with sophisticated subject tracking features that enhance its autofocus performance, making it an excellent choice for capturing moving subjects in various photography scenarios.

These features allow photographers to track subjects with precision, ensuring sharp focus and compelling compositions. Here's a detailed overview of the subject tracking capabilities of the Canon EOS R7:

1. Overview of Subject Tracking

- **Purpose**:
  - Subject tracking is designed to maintain focus on a selected subject as it moves within the frame. This is particularly useful in dynamic environments, such as sports, wildlife, and street photography, where subjects may change position quickly.

- **Continuous Autofocus**:
  - The EOS R7 utilizes continuous autofocus (AI Servo AF) in combination with its subject tracking features to keep moving subjects in focus throughout the shooting process.

2. Types of Subject Tracking

- **Face and Eye Detection Tracking**:
  - When the camera detects a human face, it can prioritize tracking the subject's face and eyes. This feature is particularly effective for portrait photography, ensuring that the subject's eyes remain sharp, even if they turn or move within the frame.

- **Animal Detection Tracking**:
  - The EOS R7 includes animal detection capabilities, allowing the camera to recognize and track the faces and eyes of animals. This is especially beneficial

for wildlife photographers, ensuring sharp focus on the subject's eyes as it moves.

- **Custom Tracking Sensitivity**:
    - The camera allows photographers to adjust tracking sensitivity, which determines how quickly the camera responds to subject movements. This is useful for adapting to different shooting situations, whether tracking fast-moving athletes or slower-moving wildlife.

3. Using Subject Tracking Features Effectively

- **Activating Subject Tracking**:
    - To utilize subject tracking, select the appropriate AF mode (typically AI Servo AF) and enable face/eye or animal detection in the camera's menu. Photographers can also customize settings to optimize tracking performance.

- **Selecting the Subject**:
    - Once subject tracking is activated, photographers can select the subject by placing the AF point over the face or body of the subject. The camera will then lock focus on that subject and maintain tracking as it moves.

- **Monitoring the Viewfinder**:
    - As you shoot, keep an eye on the viewfinder or LCD screen to ensure the camera is tracking the intended subject. The focus point indicator will show whether the camera maintains focus on the selected subject.

4. Benefits of Subject Tracking Features

- **Improved Focus Accuracy**:
    - Subject tracking enhances the accuracy of focus on moving subjects, reducing the chances of missed shots or out-of-focus images.

- **Efficiency in Fast-Paced Situations**:
    - The ability to track subjects efficiently allows photographers to capture action shots without needing to manually adjust focus constantly. This is crucial in fast-paced environments like sports or wildlife photography.

- **Creativity in Compositions**:
    - With reliable subject tracking, photographers can experiment with different compositions, knowing the camera will maintain focus on the subject, even as it moves through the frame.

- **Enhanced Shooting Experience**:
    - The intuitive subject tracking features contribute to a more enjoyable shooting experience, allowing photographers to concentrate on capturing moments without the stress of maintaining focus.

5. Limitations and Considerations

- **Lighting Conditions**:
    - While subject tracking is effective in various lighting conditions, performance may be hindered in low-light situations. In such cases, it may be beneficial to use a faster lens or increase the ISO to improve tracking capabilities.

- **Complex Backgrounds**:
    - In scenes with many moving elements or distractions in the background, the camera may occasionally lose track of the intended subject. It's essential to monitor the focus point and adjust as needed.

- **Camera Settings**:
    - Understanding the camera settings related to tracking sensitivity and AF point selection is crucial for optimizing performance. Taking the time to customize these settings can lead to better tracking results.

The subject tracking features on the Canon EOS R7 provide photographers with powerful tools to capture sharp and engaging images of moving subjects. By leveraging advanced face and eye detection, animal tracking, and customizable sensitivity settings, photographers can enhance their ability to track subjects effectively in various shooting scenarios.

Mastering these features will lead to improved photography outcomes, whether shooting fast-paced sports, wildlife, or candid moments in everyday life.

Customizing Autofocus Settings

The Canon EOS R7 offers a wide range of customizable autofocus (AF) settings, allowing photographers to tailor the camera's focus behaviour to their specific shooting needs. By understanding and adjusting these settings, you can optimize the autofocus system for various scenarios, ensuring better results and enhanced creative control.

Here's a comprehensive guide on how to customize autofocus settings on the Canon EOS R7:

1. Accessing Autofocus Settings

- **Menu Navigation**:
    - To customize autofocus settings, press the **Menu** button on the back of the camera and navigate to the **AF Menu**. Here, you will find various options related to autofocus modes, points, and functions.

2. Choosing the AF Mode

- **AF Modes**:
    - Select from various AF modes (One-Shot AF, AI Servo AF, AI Focus AF) based on your shooting situation. You can set your preferred mode directly through the AF menu or by rotating the mode dial to access your desired shooting style.

3. Customizing AF Points and Area Selection

- **AF Point Selection**:
    - Choose between various AF point selection modes (Single-point AF, Zone AF, Wide Area AF, Spot AF) based on your composition needs.
    - Use the **Multi-Controller** to quickly select the desired AF point or area. This allows for precise focus on specific subjects in different compositions.

4. Adjusting Tracking Settings

- **Tracking Sensitivity**:
    - Within the AF menu, you can adjust the **Tracking Sensitivity**, which determines how quickly the camera reacts to a subject moving in and out of the focus area. This is particularly useful when tracking fast-moving subjects or adjusting for different shooting environments.
- **Accurate Subject Tracking**:
    - Customizing tracking settings allows you to fine-tune how aggressively the camera maintains focus on a subject as it moves. This can be adjusted to be more responsive or less so, depending on the type of subjects you typically photograph.

5. Face and Eye Detection Customization

- **Face/Eye Detection Settings**:
    - Enable or disable Face and Eye Detection in the AF menu. You can also customize which eye (left or right) to prioritize when tracking a subject's face.
- **Animal Detection**:
    - Activate animal detection settings if you frequently photograph wildlife. This allows the camera to recognize and focus on the eyes of animals automatically.

6. AF Assist Features

- **AF Assist Light**:
  - The EOS R7 can use an AF assist light to improve focusing accuracy in low-light conditions. You can enable or disable this feature in the AF settings menu.

- **Lens Microadjustment**:
  - If you notice consistent focusing errors, consider performing lens microadjustment to fine-tune the autofocus performance for specific lenses. This can be done in the camera's menu under the **Lens Correction** settings.

7. Setting AF-ON Button Customization

- **Customizing the AF-ON Button**:
  - You can customize the **AF-ON** button (or other buttons) for quick access to autofocus settings. This is particularly useful for quickly switching between different AF modes or activating specific functions without navigating the menu.

8. Saving Custom AF Settings

- **Custom Shooting Modes**:
  - The EOS R7 allows you to save your customized AF settings to a custom shooting mode (C1, C2, C3) on the mode dial. This makes it easy to switch between different autofocus configurations tailored for specific shooting scenarios.

9. Testing and Fine-Tuning

- **Real-World Testing**:
  - After customizing your autofocus settings, take the time to test them in various shooting conditions. This will help you assess whether the settings meet your needs and allow for any necessary adjustments.

- **Continuous Adjustments**:
  - Autofocus preferences may change based on your shooting style, subject types, and environments. Regularly revisiting and adjusting these settings ensures that your camera is always optimized for the situation at hand.

Customizing autofocus settings on the Canon EOS R7 allows photographers to enhance their shooting experience and improve focus accuracy in various situations. By taking advantage of the extensive customization options available, you can tailor the autofocus system to suit your specific needs, whether shooting portraits, wildlife, sports, or everyday moments.

Mastering these settings will significantly improve your ability to capture sharp and compelling images in any shooting environment.

CHAPTER SEVEN
SHOOTING STILL PHOTOS

Shooting in RAW vs JPEG

When using the Canon EOS R7, one of the key decisions photographers face is whether to shoot in RAW or JPEG format. Each format has its advantages and disadvantages, and the choice ultimately depends on your shooting style, post-processing workflow, and intended use for the images.

Here's a detailed comparison of RAW and JPEG formats:

1. Overview of RAW and JPEG Formats

- **RAW**:
  - RAW files are unprocessed and contain all the data captured by the camera's sensor. They offer greater flexibility in post-processing, allowing photographers to make extensive adjustments to exposure, colour balance, and sharpness without losing image quality.

- **JPEG**:
  - JPEG files are processed and compressed versions of images. They are ready for immediate use and are smaller in file size, making them easier to share and store. However, JPEGs are limited in terms of post-processing adjustments since some data is discarded during compression.

2. Advantages of Shooting in RAW

- **Image Quality**:
  - RAW files retain all sensor data, resulting in higher image quality and detail. This is particularly beneficial for high-contrast scenes or when shooting in challenging lighting conditions.

- **Post-Processing Flexibility**:
  - RAW files allow for extensive adjustments in post-processing software, including:
    - **Exposure correction**: Recovering highlights and shadows.
    - **White balance adjustments**: Changing colour temperature without degrading quality.
    - **Dynamic range enhancement**: Extracting more detail from highlights and shadows.

- **Lossless Editing**:
    - Editing a RAW file does not affect the original data, meaning you can revert to the original image at any time, unlike JPEGs, where repeated edits can degrade quality.
- **Higher Bit Depth**:
    - RAW files typically have a higher bit depth (12 or 14 bits), allowing for smoother gradients and more precise colour representation compared to JPEGs (usually 8 bits).

3. Advantages of Shooting in JPEG

- **File Size**:
    - JPEG files are smaller due to compression, making them easier to store and share. This is particularly advantageous for photographers with limited storage space or those who need to shoot a high volume of images quickly.
- **Speed**:
    - JPEGs can be processed and saved faster than RAW files, allowing for quicker shooting bursts and reduced camera lag, which is beneficial in fast-paced shooting situations.
- **Immediate Usability**:
    - JPEGs are ready to use straight out of the camera, making them ideal for photographers who need to share images quickly, such as event photographers or journalists.
- **Compatibility**:
    - JPEG files are widely supported and can be opened on virtually any device or software without the need for specialized processing software.

4. Considerations for Shooting in RAW vs. JPEG

- **Post-Processing Needs**:
    - If you enjoy post-processing your images and want the highest quality and flexibility, shooting in RAW is the better choice. Conversely, if you prefer minimal editing and need to deliver images quickly, JPEG may be more suitable.
- **Shooting Style**:
    - For casual photography or events where speed and convenience are essential, JPEG may be the preferred format. However, for landscape, portrait, or fine art

photography, RAW is often favoured for its superior quality and editing capabilities.

- **Storage and Workflow**:
    - RAW files require more storage space, so consider your storage capacity and workflow. If you frequently run out of space or need to manage large quantities of files, JPEG may help streamline your workflow.

- **Editing Software**:
    - Ensure you have the right software to edit RAW files, as they require specific programs (like Adobe Lightroom, Photoshop, or Canon's Digital Photo Professional) to open and edit. JPEGs can be edited in virtually any image editing software.

Both RAW and JPEG formats have their unique benefits, and the choice between them depends on your photography style, post-processing preferences, and specific shooting scenarios. The Canon EOS R7 offers the flexibility to choose either format, allowing photographers to tailor their workflow to their individual needs.

For the best image quality and editing flexibility, RAW is often the preferred option, while JPEG may be more suitable for fast-paced environments or when immediate usability is essential. Ultimately, understanding the strengths and limitations of each format will help you make informed decisions for your photography.

Burst Shooting and Continuous Mode

The Canon EOS R7 features advanced burst shooting and continuous mode capabilities, making it an excellent choice for capturing fast-moving subjects and action scenes. These modes allow photographers to take multiple shots in quick succession, ensuring they don't miss critical moments. Here's an in-depth look at burst shooting and continuous mode on the Canon EOS R7:

1. Overview of Burst Shooting and Continuous Mode

- **Burst Shooting**:
    - Burst shooting refers to the ability to take a series of images in rapid succession by holding down the shutter button. This mode is ideal for capturing fast action, sports, wildlife, and candid moments.

- **Continuous Mode**:
    - Continuous mode is a specific setting that allows the camera to take photos continuously as long as the shutter button is pressed. The EOS R7 offers different speeds for continuous shooting, giving photographers flexibility depending on the shooting scenario.

2. Burst Shooting Capabilities of the EOS R7

- **Frame Rate**:
    - The EOS R7 can shoot at impressive frame rates, with options for up to **30 frames per second (fps)** when using the electronic shutter. This high frame rate is beneficial for capturing rapid movements, such as sports or wildlife in action.

- **Mechanical Shutter**:
    - When using the mechanical shutter, the EOS R7 can achieve burst shooting speeds of up to **15 fps**. This is suitable for various shooting situations while providing the benefits of the mechanical shutter's distinct sound and performance.

- **RAW and JPEG Options**:
    - Burst shooting can be performed in both RAW and JPEG formats, although continuous shooting in RAW may result in buffer limitations depending on the camera's storage capacity and the speed of the memory card being used.

3. Continuous Shooting Modes

- **Continuous AF (AI Servo AF)**:
    - In continuous shooting mode, the EOS R7 utilizes AI Servo AF to track moving subjects. This ensures that the camera maintains focus on the subject throughout the burst, providing sharp images even as the subject moves.

- **Focus Priority and Release Priority**:
    - Photographers can customize the continuous shooting settings to prioritize either focus accuracy or the speed of shutter release. In **Focus Priority**, the camera will wait for focus to be achieved before firing, while in **Release Priority**, it will take photos as quickly as possible, regardless of focus.

4. Using Burst Shooting and Continuous Mode Effectively

- **Selecting the Mode**:
    - To enable burst shooting, rotate the mode dial to **Shooting Mode** (such as **P, Av, Tv, or M**) and set the camera to continuous shooting mode in the menu. Choose the desired frame rate based on the action and available light.

- **Focusing Settings**:
    - Set the autofocus mode to **AI Servo AF** to ensure the camera continually adjusts focus during the burst. This is especially important for tracking moving subjects effectively.

- **Timing and Composition**:
    - Use burst shooting to capture sequences of action. Consider the timing and composition to frame your shots correctly. This is useful in scenarios like sports photography or capturing candid moments in social settings.
- **Memory Card Considerations**:
    - Ensure you use a high-speed memory card (UHS-II or faster) to handle the large file sizes and fast write speeds associated with burst shooting. This helps prevent buffering issues and allows for uninterrupted shooting.

5. Limitations and Considerations

- **Buffer Limitations**:
    - While burst shooting allows for rapid firing of images, the camera has a limited buffer size. Shooting in RAW will fill the buffer more quickly than JPEG. Be mindful of this, especially during extended bursts.
- **Battery Life**:
    - Continuous shooting can consume battery power rapidly. Consider carrying spare batteries for longer shooting sessions, especially during events or outdoor activities.
- **Post-Processing**:
    - Be prepared for post-processing, as burst shooting can result in numerous images to sift through. Developing a workflow for organizing and editing burst images will help streamline your post-shooting process.

The burst shooting and continuous mode capabilities of the Canon EOS R7 provide photographers with powerful tools to capture fast action and dynamic moments. With impressive frame rates, continuous autofocus, and customizable shooting options, this camera excels in situations where timing is crucial.

By understanding how to effectively utilize these features, photographers can enhance their ability to capture compelling images, whether in sports, wildlife, or everyday candid moments.

Using the Electronic Shutter

The Canon EOS R7 features an electronic shutter option, which allows photographers to capture images without the mechanical movement of a traditional shutter. This mode offers unique benefits, particularly in specific shooting scenarios. Here's a detailed guide on using the electronic shutter on the Canon EOS R7:

1. Overview of the Electronic Shutter

- **Functionality**:
  - The electronic shutter uses electronic signals to capture images, eliminating the need for physical shutter blades. This allows for silent operation and enables faster shutter speeds than a mechanical shutter can achieve.

- **Silent Shooting**:
  - One of the main advantages of the electronic shutter is its silent shooting capability. This is particularly useful in environments where noise may be disruptive, such as during weddings, wildlife photography, or in quiet settings like museums.

2. Benefits of Using the Electronic Shutter

- **Fast Shutter Speeds**:
  - The electronic shutter can achieve very fast shutter speeds, up to **1/32,000 of a second**. This capability is beneficial for freezing fast action, such as in sports or wildlife photography, and for shooting in bright conditions without overexposing the image.

- **Reduced Camera Shake**:
  - With no mechanical movement involved, the risk of camera shake is minimized, allowing for sharper images, particularly at slower shutter speeds.

- **Expanded Shooting Opportunities**:
  - The silent operation and fast speeds make the electronic shutter ideal for unique photography opportunities, such as capturing fleeting moments in dynamic environments without disturbing the subject.

3. Setting Up the Electronic Shutter

- **Accessing the Electronic Shutter**:
  - To enable the electronic shutter, navigate to the **Menu** and select the **Shooting Settings**. Within the shutter settings, you can choose between mechanical and electronic shutter options.

- **Switching Between Shutter Types**:
    - The EOS R7 allows you to switch between the electronic and mechanical shutter modes easily. Consider using the electronic shutter for specific scenarios, such as quiet environments or fast-paced action.

4. Using the Electronic Shutter Effectively

- **Selecting Shooting Modes**:
    - The electronic shutter is compatible with various shooting modes (P, Av, Tv, M). Depending on your subject and shooting environment, choose the appropriate mode for your needs.

- **Adjusting Exposure Settings**:
    - When using the electronic shutter, pay attention to exposure settings, especially in bright conditions. You may need to adjust your aperture and ISO to avoid overexposure, particularly when using fast shutter speeds.

- **Continuous Shooting**:
    - The electronic shutter can be used in continuous shooting mode, allowing for burst shooting at high frame rates (up to 30 fps). This is advantageous for capturing fast action, but be aware of potential rolling shutter effects.

5. Considerations and Limitations

- **Rolling Shutter Effect**:
    - One of the primary limitations of the electronic shutter is the potential for rolling shutter distortion, especially with fast-moving subjects or rapid camera movements. This can lead to distortion in the captured image, particularly in dynamic scenes.

- **Lighting Conditions**:
    - The electronic shutter may not perform well in certain lighting conditions, particularly with artificial lighting (like fluorescent or LED lights). This can result in banding or flickering in the images. Testing and adjusting settings in such environments may be necessary.

- **Battery Consumption**:
    - While the electronic shutter is generally efficient, continuous shooting with high frame rates may lead to quicker battery drain. Carrying spare batteries can help during long shooting sessions.

6. Practical Applications of the Electronic Shutter

- **Wildlife Photography**:
    - The silent operation of the electronic shutter allows photographers to capture images of skittish wildlife without startling the animals.
- **Event Photography**:
    - In settings such as weddings or performances, the ability to shoot silently helps capture candid moments without being intrusive.
- **Sports Photography**:
    - The fast shutter speeds available with the electronic shutter enable photographers to freeze action in high-speed sports, making it easier to capture the peak moment of the action.

The electronic shutter on the Canon EOS R7 provides photographers with a valuable tool for capturing images in a variety of situations. With its silent operation, fast shutter speeds, and reduced risk of camera shake, the electronic shutter excels in environments where traditional shutter sounds may be disruptive or when speed is essential.

Understanding how to set up and use the electronic shutter effectively will enhance your ability to capture compelling images, whether in wildlife, events, or fast-paced sports photography.

Understanding Exposure (ISO, Aperture, Shutter Speed)

Exposure is a fundamental concept in photography, determining how light or dark an image appears. It is controlled by three key elements: ISO, aperture, and shutter speed. Understanding how these three components work together, often referred to as the Exposure Triangle, is crucial for mastering photography with the Canon EOS R7. Here's a detailed breakdown of each element:

1. ISO (International Standards Organization)

- **Definition**:
    - ISO measures the camera's sensitivity to light. A higher ISO value means greater sensitivity, allowing you to capture images in lower light conditions, but it can introduce noise or grain in the image.
- **ISO Settings**:
    - The EOS R7 typically offers a range of ISO settings, often from **100 to 32,000**, with the possibility of extending it to **50 and 51,200** in certain modes.
- **When to Adjust ISO**:
    - Increase ISO in low-light situations (e.g., indoors, at night, or in shadowy environments).
    - Use lower ISO settings in bright conditions (e.g., sunny days) to avoid overexposure and maintain image quality.

- **Considerations**:
  - While higher ISO allows for better performance in low light, it can lead to increased noise. Finding a balance between ISO and other exposure settings is key.

2. Aperture

- **Definition**:
  - Aperture refers to the opening in the lens through which light enters the camera. It is measured in **f-stops** (e.g., f/2.8, f/4, f/8). A lower f-stop number indicates a larger opening, allowing lighter to enter, while a higher f-stop number indicates a smaller opening.

- **Impact on Exposure**:
  - A wider aperture (e.g., f/2.8) allows more light to hit the sensor, resulting in a brighter image. Conversely, a smaller aperture (e.g., f/16) lets in less light, resulting in a darker image.

- **Depth of Field**:
  - Aperture also affects the depth of field (DoF), or how much of the image is in focus.
    - A wide aperture (lower f-stop) creates a shallow depth of field, blurring the background and isolating the subject.
    - A narrow aperture (higher f-stop) results in a greater depth of field, keeping more of the scene in focus, which is ideal for landscapes.

- **When to Adjust Aperture**:
  - Use a wide aperture for portrait photography to achieve a blurred background.
  - Use a narrow aperture for landscape photography to ensure more elements are in focus.

3. Shutter Speed

- **Definition**:
  - Shutter speed refers to the amount of time the camera's shutter is open, allowing light to reach the sensor. It is measured in seconds (e.g., 1/1000, 1/60, 2 seconds).

- **Impact on Exposure**:
  - A fast shutter speed (e.g., 1/1000) lets in less light, resulting in a darker image. A slow shutter speed (e.g., 1 second) allows more light in, resulting in a brighter image.

- **Motion Blur**:
    - Shutter speed also influences motion blur:
        - Fast shutter speeds freeze action (ideal for sports or wildlife photography).
        - Slow shutter speeds create motion blur (useful for artistic effects or to capture movement in water).
- **When to Adjust Shutter Speed**:
    - Use a fast shutter speed to freeze fast-moving subjects (e.g., during a race).
    - Use a slow shutter speed to create a sense of motion (e.g., flowing water).

4. Balancing the Exposure Triangle

- **Interdependence**:
    - The three elements of the exposure triangle are interconnected. Adjusting one element will require adjustments to the others to maintain proper exposure.
        - For example, if you increase ISO to capture a photo in low light, you may need to decrease aperture or shorten shutter speed to avoid overexposure.
- **Exposure Compensation**:
    - The EOS R7 features an exposure compensation function that allows you to adjust the exposure without changing the camera's exposure settings manually. This is useful for fine-tuning exposure in tricky lighting situations.
- **Histogram and Metering**:
    - Use the camera's histogram and metering modes to assess exposure. The histogram displays the distribution of light in your image, helping you avoid underexposed (clipped shadows) or overexposed (clipped highlights) areas.

5. Practical Applications

- **Shooting in Manual Mode**:
    - Experimenting with manual mode on the EOS R7 can help you understand how ISO, aperture, and shutter speed work together. Start with one setting and adjust the others to achieve your desired exposure.
- **Creative Photography**:
    - Use the exposure triangle creatively to achieve specific effects. For instance, you might choose a slow shutter speed and wide aperture for dreamy images of moving water or a wide aperture for portraits with beautiful bokeh.

Understanding exposure through ISO, aperture, and shutter speed is vital for mastering photography with the Canon EOS R7. Each element plays a significant role in determining the overall brightness and quality of your images.

By learning how to balance these settings, photographers can gain greater creative control, adapt to various lighting conditions, and capture stunning images.

CHAPTER EIGHT
SHOOTING VIDEOS

Video Recording Options

The Canon EOS R7 is designed not just for photography but also excels in video recording capabilities, making it a versatile choice for content creators. With various settings and options, the R7 allows users to capture high-quality video footage in different resolutions, frame rates, and formats. Here's a detailed guide on the video recording options available on the Canon EOS R7:

1. Video Resolutions and Frame Rates

- **4K Video Recording**:
    - The EOS R7 supports 4K video recording at multiple frame rates:
        - Up to **60 fps** (frames per second) in **4K** using the full width of the sensor.
        - Up to **120 fps** in **4K** with a crop factor (approximately 1.5x).
    - 4K video offers excellent detail and clarity, suitable for professional video projects.

- **Full HD (1080p) Recording**:
    - Full HD recording is available at various frame rates:
        - Up to **120 fps** for slow-motion effects.
        - Standard frame rates such as **24 fps**, **30 fps**, and **60 fps** for typical video projects.
    - This flexibility allows creators to choose the right frame rate based on the desired look of the video.

- **HD (720p) Recording**:
    - The camera also supports **720p** video recording, which can be useful for lower-resolution applications or when file sizes need to be minimized.

2. Video Formats and Compression

- **File Formats**:
    - The EOS R7 records video in two primary formats:
        - **MP4**: A widely compatible format that balances quality and file size, suitable for most editing applications.
        - **ALL-I**: An intra-frame compression format that offers higher quality and less compression for more flexibility in post-production. This is ideal for professional workflows.

- **Bit Rate**:
    - o The camera supports high bit rates for 4K video, providing better image quality and detail. Bit rates can go up to **240 Mbps** in 4K recording, ensuring rich video quality.

3. Video Features and Settings

- **Dual Pixel CMOS AF**:
    - o The Canon EOS R7 utilizes **Dual Pixel Autofocus** for smooth and accurate focusing during video recording. This feature ensures that subjects remain sharp and in focus, even during movement.

- **Focus Breathing Compensation**:
    - o This feature helps reduce focus breathing during zooms and focus changes, maintaining a consistent field of view, which is particularly beneficial for filmmakers.

- **V-Log and Canon Log**:
    - o The EOS R7 supports **Canon Log 3** for improved dynamic range and color grading flexibility in post-production. This feature is particularly useful for professional videographers seeking high-quality footage.

- **Built-in Stabilization**:
    - o The camera includes **Electronic Image Stabilization (EIS)**, which helps to reduce camera shake and produces smoother footage, especially when shooting handheld.

4. Audio Recording Options

- **Microphone Input**:
    - o The EOS R7 features a **3.5mm microphone input** for external microphones, allowing for higher-quality audio recording compared to the built-in microphone.

- **Headphone Jack**:
    - o A **3.5mm headphone jack** is also included for monitoring audio levels in real-time during recording, ensuring that sound quality meets the desired standards.

5. **Other Considerations**

- **Overheating Management**:
    - The Canon EOS R7 has features in place to manage heat during prolonged video recording sessions, which is crucial for maintaining performance during extended shoots.

- **Recording Limits**:
    - There are recording limits based on the resolution and frame rate chosen. For example, in 4K at 60 fps, the camera may have a limit of **30 minutes** of continuous recording.

- **Battery Life**:
    - Video recording can drain the battery more quickly than still photography. Using a high-capacity battery or a power adapter for extended shoots is advisable.

The video recording options on the Canon EOS R7 offer a comprehensive range of settings for both amateur and professional videographers. With its 4K capabilities, various frame rates, high-quality audio options, and advanced autofocus features, the EOS R7 is well-suited for creating dynamic video content.

Understanding and utilizing these options will enhance your ability to capture high-quality video that meets your creative vision.

4K Video and Frame Rates

The Canon EOS R7 is a powerful mirrorless camera that offers robust 4K video recording capabilities, making it an excellent choice for videographers and content creators. Understanding the specifics of 4K video and frame rates will help you make the most of this camera's video features. Here's a detailed overview of 4K video options and frame rates available on the EOS R7:

1. 4K Video Resolution

- **Definition**:
    - 4K video, also known as Ultra High Definition (UHD), has a resolution of **3840 x 2160 pixels**, providing four times the detail of Full HD (1080p). This higher resolution allows for greater detail and clarity, making it ideal for professional video work.

- **Benefits**:
    - The increased resolution allows for larger prints, better cropping flexibility, and improved detail in scenes, which is essential for high-quality video production.

2. Frame Rates for 4K Video

The EOS R7 offers a variety of frame rates for 4K video recording, allowing filmmakers to choose the best option for their creative needs:

- **Standard Frame Rates**:
    - **24 fps**: The standard frame rate for cinematic video, providing a film-like look. Ideal for narrative filmmaking and most video projects.
    - **30 fps**: Common for broadcast television and online content. It offers a slightly smoother motion compared to 24 fps.
    - **60 fps**: Useful for sports and fast-paced action, providing smoother motion and allowing for slow-motion playback when downsampled.
- **High Frame Rate Options**:
    - **120 fps**: Available in **4K** but with a crop factor. This setting allows for slow-motion effects in 4K footage, enabling filmmakers to capture fast-moving subjects and create dramatic, slow-motion sequences.
    - **240 fps**: This is not available in 4K but can be used in **Full HD (1080p)** mode, offering even more dramatic slow-motion capabilities.

3. Crop Factor Considerations

- **Crop in 4K**:
    - When recording at **120 fps** in 4K, the camera applies a crop to the image sensor, approximately 1.5x. This means that the field of view will be narrower, affecting composition and framing.
    - It's essential to account for this crop factor when choosing your lens and planning your shots, especially in tight spaces or when trying to capture wide scenes.

4. Video Quality Settings

- **Bit Rate**:
    - The EOS R7 supports high bit rates for 4K video recording, ensuring better image quality. Bit rates can reach up to **240 Mbps**, providing more detail and colour depth in your footage.
- **File Format**:
    - The camera records 4K video primarily in the **MP4** format, which is widely compatible and suitable for most editing software. It also offers **ALL-I** compression for those who require higher quality and more flexibility in post-production.

5. Practical Applications of 4K Video and Frame Rates

- **Cinematic Productions**:
    - Use 24 fps for a traditional film look in narrative storytelling or short films.

- **Documentaries and Online Content**:
    - 30 fps can be ideal for documentary filmmaking and content aimed at online audiences, providing a good balance between smooth motion and cinematic feel.

- **Action and Sports**:
    - Utilize 60 fps or 120 fps when capturing fast-paced action, such as sports events, to ensure clear, smooth footage that can also be slowed down for dramatic effect.

- **Creative Slow Motion**:
    - Use the high frame rate options (120 fps in 4K) to capture moments that are too fast for the human eye, such as sports highlights or dynamic movements, adding a dramatic flair to your videos.

The 4K video capabilities of the Canon EOS R7 offer a range of frame rates and settings that cater to various videography needs. Whether you're shooting cinematic films, documentaries, or action-packed events, understanding how to utilize these options effectively will enhance your video production quality.

The combination of high resolution, versatile frame rates, and advanced recording features makes the EOS R7 a powerful tool for any videographer.

Autofocus for Video Recording

The Canon EOS R7 features advanced autofocus systems that significantly enhance video recording capabilities. Autofocus is critical in videography, ensuring that subjects remain sharp and in focus throughout a shot.

Here's a detailed overview of the autofocus options available for video recording on the Canon EOS R7:

1. Dual Pixel CMOS AF Technology

- **Definition**:
    - The Canon EOS R7 is equipped with **Dual Pixel CMOS AF**, a sophisticated autofocus technology that allows for fast and accurate focusing. Each pixel on the sensor has dual photodiodes that enable phase detection focusing.

- **Advantages**:
    - **Speed and Accuracy**: Dual Pixel AF provides smooth and precise focus transitions, making it ideal for moving subjects in video.

- **Real-Time Tracking**: The system can track subjects continuously as they move, maintaining sharp focus throughout the shot.

2. AF Modes for Video

The EOS R7 offers various autofocus modes tailored for different shooting scenarios:

- **One-Shot AF**:
  - Primarily used for still photography, this mode locks focus when the shutter button is pressed halfway. In video, it can be useful for static subjects.
- **Servo AF**:
  - This mode continuously adjusts focus while recording, making it ideal for moving subjects. It ensures that the focus remains locked on the subject as it moves within the frame.
- **Face Detection AF**:
  - The camera can automatically detect and focus on human faces, which is particularly useful in interview settings or when capturing people in motion.
- **Eye Detection AF**:
  - This feature prioritizes focusing on the subject's eyes, providing a more intimate and focused framing, especially in portraits and interviews.

3. Focus Area Options

The EOS R7 provides several options for selecting focus areas during video recording:

- **Single Point AF**:
  - Allows the user to select a specific focus point, giving precise control over where the camera focuses.
- **Zone AF**:
  - This mode allows for a group of focus points to be selected, useful for tracking subjects within a specific area of the frame.
- **Wide Area AF**:
  - The camera automatically selects focus points over a wide area, useful for unpredictable movements.
- **Tracking AF**:
  - This mode locks onto a selected subject and follows it as it moves within the frame, ensuring it remains in focus.

4. Focus Breathing Compensation

- **What It Is**:
  - Focus breathing refers to the phenomenon where the field of view changes slightly when adjusting focus, often noticeable during rack focusing (shifting focus from one subject to another).
- **Feature in R7**:
  - The EOS R7 includes a focus breathing compensation feature that minimizes this effect, providing smoother transitions and maintaining a consistent composition while focusing.

5. Manual Focus Override

- **Manual Control**:
  - Users can switch to manual focus while recording if preferred, allowing for precise control over focus adjustments. The focus ring can be easily adjusted for critical focus on desired subjects.
- **Focus Peaking**:
  - The camera offers focus peaking, which highlights the areas in focus, making it easier to achieve precise manual focus, particularly useful in situations with shallow depth of field.

6. Recording Settings and Autofocus Performance

- **Autofocus Speed**:
  - The EOS R7 features customizable autofocus speed settings, allowing users to adjust how quickly the camera transitions focus between subjects.
- **Sensitivity Settings**:
  - Autofocus sensitivity can also be adjusted to ensure it responds appropriately to different scenarios, such as rapid movements or subtle changes in subject position.

The autofocus system on the Canon EOS R7 is designed to enhance the videography experience, providing fast, accurate, and reliable focusing capabilities. With features like Dual Pixel CMOS AF, various autofocus modes, and focus breathing compensation, the R7 allows videographers to capture dynamic and engaging footage with ease.

Understanding and utilizing these autofocus options can greatly improve the quality of your video recordings and ensure that your subjects remain sharp and in focus throughout your projects.

Stabilization Features for Smooth Video

The Canon EOS R7 is equipped with several stabilization features that help deliver smooth, shake-free video recordings, making it an ideal choice for videographers and content creators. Here's a comprehensive overview of the stabilization options available on the R7:

1. In-Body Image Stabilization (IBIS)

- **What It Is**: The EOS R7 features In-Body Image Stabilization (IBIS), which compensates for camera shake by physically shifting the camera's sensor. This system works in conjunction with the lens stabilization to enhance overall stabilization performance.

- **Benefits**:

    o **Enhanced Stability**: IBIS provides stabilization for all types of shooting, especially beneficial when shooting handheld or in situations where using a tripod isn't practical.

    o **Versatility**: Effective across various video formats and resolutions, including 4K, making it suitable for a wide range of shooting conditions.

2. Electronic Image Stabilization (EIS)

- **Definition**: The R7 also offers Electronic Image Stabilization (EIS), which is applied during video recording to further reduce shake and vibration. EIS works by cropping the video frame slightly and compensating for camera movement electronically.

- **Functionality**:

    o When activated, EIS allows for even smoother footage, especially during dynamic movements, such as walking or running while filming.

    o EIS is particularly effective for video content where maximum stability is desired, such as vlogs, action shots, or run-and-gun filming scenarios.

3. Combination of IBIS and EIS

- **Hybrid Stabilization**: When used together, IBIS and EIS provide a powerful stabilization solution that significantly reduces camera shake and vibrations. This combination is especially useful for handheld shooting in challenging conditions.

- **Practical Application**:

    o The hybrid stabilization system enables videographers to achieve smooth, cinematic shots even when moving quickly or navigating uneven terrain.

4. Focus on Video Modes

- **4K and Full HD Stability**:
    - Both 4K and Full HD video recordings benefit from the stabilization features, with the R7 maintaining smooth footage regardless of the resolution selected.
    - When using high frame rates (e.g., 120 fps) in 4K, the stabilization remains effective, allowing for clear and stable slow-motion footage.

5. Shooting Techniques for Enhanced Stabilization

- **Use of Lenses with Optical Stabilization**:
    - In addition to the camera's IBIS, using RF or compatible EF lenses with **Optical Image Stabilization (OIS)** can further enhance stabilization. This dual approach provides a greater degree of shake reduction.

- **Stabilization Modes**:
    - The R7 allows users to choose from different stabilization modes, which can be tailored based on the shooting situation (e.g., standard stabilization for general use or enhanced stabilization for more dynamic movements).

- **Practice Good Handheld Techniques**:
    - Employing good handheld shooting techniques, such as keeping the elbows close to the body and using a stable stance, can complement the camera's stabilization features.

6. Limitations and Considerations

- **Crop Factor**:
    - When using EIS, a slight crop is applied to the video frame, which may affect composition. It's important to consider this crop when framing shots, particularly in wide-angle scenes.

- **Battery Life**:
    - Activating stabilization features may consume additional battery power, so it's advisable to monitor battery life during extended shooting sessions.

The stabilization features of the Canon EOS R7—including In-Body Image Stabilization (IBIS) and Electronic Image Stabilization (EIS)—are designed to provide smooth and professional-quality video recordings. Whether you're capturing fast-paced action or filming vlogs, these stabilization technologies ensure that your footage remains steady and visually appealing.

Understanding how to leverage these features, along with proper shooting techniques, will enhance your videography and enable you to create engaging content with ease.

CHAPTER NINE
ADVANCED FEATURES OF CANON EOS R7

In-Body Image Stabilization (IBIS)

In-Body Image Stabilization (IBIS) is a key feature of the Canon EOS R7 that enhances the camera's ability to capture sharp images and smooth videos, even in challenging shooting conditions. Here's a detailed overview of how IBIS works and its benefits for photographers and videographers.

1. How IBIS Works

- **Mechanism**:
  - IBIS compensates for camera shake by physically shifting the camera's image sensor. It employs gyroscopic sensors to detect movement in real-time and adjusts the position of the sensor to counteract any unwanted motion, whether it's caused by handheld shooting, walking, or other vibrations.

- **Axis Stabilization**:
  - The EOS R7 features stabilization across **five axes**:
    - **Yaw** (horizontal rotation)
    - **Pitch** (vertical rotation)
    - **Roll** (tilting)
    - **X-axis** (horizontal shift)
    - **Y-axis** (vertical shift)
  - This comprehensive stabilization helps to mitigate various forms of camera shake, resulting in clearer images and smoother video footage.

2. Benefits of IBIS

- **Improved Low-Light Performance**:
  - IBIS allows for slower shutter speeds without the risk of motion blur, making it easier to shoot in low-light conditions. Photographers can capture clear images in dim environments without needing a tripod.

- **Smoother Video Recording**:
  - For videographers, IBIS is invaluable in providing stable footage, reducing the need for external stabilization equipment like gimbals. This feature is especially beneficial for handheld shooting and dynamic scenes.

- **Enhanced Composition Flexibility**:
  - With the ability to shoot at slower shutter speeds, photographers have more creative freedom to use wide apertures for depth of field or capture motion blur effects without sacrificing sharpness.
- **Compatibility with Various Lenses**:
  - IBIS works effectively with both RF and EF lenses, enhancing stabilization even when using lenses without built-in optical stabilization.

3. Using IBIS Effectively

- **Activate IBIS**:
  - Ensure that the IBIS feature is enabled in the camera settings before shooting. The R7 allows users to customize stabilization settings based on their shooting preferences.
- **Combine with Lens Stabilization**:
  - For optimal performance, use RF or compatible EF lenses that feature Optical Image Stabilization (OIS). The combination of IBIS and OIS can provide even greater shake reduction.
- **Shooting Techniques**:
  - While IBIS significantly reduces shake, employing good handheld shooting techniques—such as keeping elbows close to the body, using a stable stance, and breathing control—can enhance the effectiveness of stabilization.

4. Limitations of IBIS

- **Crop Factor**:
  - While IBIS is effective, using certain video recording settings may involve cropping the frame, which can affect composition. Be mindful of this when framing shots, especially in wide-angle scenes.
- **Battery Life**:
  - Utilizing IBIS may slightly impact battery life during extended shooting sessions. Monitoring battery levels is advisable, especially in long shoots.
- **Effectiveness**:
  - While IBIS is highly effective for compensating for small movements, extreme vibrations (such as those from rapid running or heavy machinery) may still require additional stabilization equipment.

In-Body Image Stabilization (IBIS) on the Canon EOS R7 is a powerful feature that enhances both photography and videography.

By effectively reducing camera shake and providing stable images and videos, IBIS allows photographers and videographers to capture high-quality content in a variety of shooting conditions. Understanding how to leverage this technology can significantly improve your shooting experience and the overall quality of your work.

Dual Pixel RAW

Dual Pixel RAW is an innovative feature offered by the Canon EOS R7 that enhances the creative possibilities for photographers, particularly in post-processing. This technology allows users to capture images with more depth and detail, making it easier to adjust focus and enhance the overall quality of photos.

Here's a detailed overview of Dual Pixel RAW, its functionality, and its benefits.

1. What is Dual Pixel RAW?

- **Definition**: Dual Pixel RAW captures images using the camera's Dual Pixel CMOS AF technology, recording two separate images for each shot. This feature provides additional data that can be used during post-processing.

- **Mechanism**:
    - When Dual Pixel RAW is enabled, the camera captures a standard RAW image along with a secondary RAW image that contains slightly different information. This allows for advanced editing options in post-processing.

2. Key Features of Dual Pixel RAW

- **Focus Adjustment**:
    - One of the standout features of Dual Pixel RAW is the ability to slightly adjust the focus point after the image has been captured. This is particularly useful for portraits or macro photography, where precise focus is critical.

- **Background and Foreground Control**:
    - The technology allows photographers to adjust the bokeh effect in an image. Users can choose to enhance the background blur or maintain focus on foreground elements, providing more creative control over the depth of field.

- **Improved HDR Processing**:
    - Dual Pixel RAW can assist in creating high dynamic range (HDR) images. By capturing additional data, it helps in preserving details in both highlights and shadows during post-processing.

3. How to Use Dual Pixel RAW

- **Enable Dual Pixel RAW**:
    - To use Dual Pixel RAW, you need to enable the feature in the camera settings. This setting can usually be found in the menu under the image quality options.

- **Shooting with Dual Pixel RAW**:
    - When shooting, ensure that the camera is set to capture in RAW format. The file size will be larger due to the additional data being recorded.

- **Post-Processing Software**:
    - To take advantage of Dual Pixel RAW, you'll need to use compatible software, such as Canon's Digital Photo Professional (DPP) or other advanced RAW editing programs that support Dual Pixel RAW features.

4. Benefits of Dual Pixel RAW

- **Creative Flexibility**:
    - Photographers gain greater flexibility in post-processing, allowing for adjustments to focus and depth of field that can enhance the final image.

- **Enhanced Image Quality**:
    - By recording two sets of data, Dual Pixel RAW helps to preserve more details, resulting in images with better clarity and dynamic range.

- **Error Correction**:
    - In situations where focus may not be perfect, the ability to adjust focus after the fact can save shots that might otherwise be unusable.

5. Limitations of Dual Pixel RAW

- **File Size**:
    - Dual Pixel RAW files are larger than standard RAW files due to the additional data being captured. This can impact storage requirements and processing time.

- **Processing Time**:
    - The need for advanced processing to take full advantage of Dual Pixel RAW may require additional time in post-production, especially for those unfamiliar with the technology.

- **Not Ideal for Every Situation**:
    - While Dual Pixel RAW is beneficial for specific types of photography, such as portraits or macro shots, it may not be necessary for every scenario. Photographers should evaluate whether the added complexity is worthwhile for their particular shoot.

Dual Pixel RAW on the Canon EOS R7 is a powerful feature that enhances the creative control photographers have over their images. By allowing adjustments to focus and depth of field in post-processing, it opens up new possibilities for capturing high-quality, detailed images.

Understanding how to effectively use Dual Pixel RAW can significantly elevate your photography, providing you with the tools to achieve your artistic vision.

High-Speed Shooting

High-Speed Shooting is a prominent feature of the Canon EOS R7 that allows photographers to capture fast-moving subjects with precision and clarity. This capability is especially beneficial for sports, wildlife, and action photography, where timing is crucial.

Here's a comprehensive overview of high-speed shooting, its features, and how to make the most of it with the EOS R7.

1. Burst Shooting Capabilities

- **Continuous Shooting Rate**: The EOS R7 offers an impressive continuous shooting speed of up to **15 frames per second (fps)** using the mechanical shutter and up to **30 fps** with the electronic shutter. This allows photographers to capture rapid sequences of images, ensuring they don't miss critical moments.
- **Silent Shooting**: When using the electronic shutter, the EOS R7 operates silently, making it ideal for environments where noise may be a concern, such as wildlife photography or events.

2. AF Performance During High-Speed Shooting

- **Dual Pixel AF**:
    - The EOS R7 utilizes **Dual Pixel CMOS AF**, which provides fast and accurate autofocus performance even during high-speed shooting. This technology ensures that the subject remains in focus, even as it moves quickly within the frame.
- **Subject Tracking**:
    - The camera's advanced subject tracking capabilities allow it to maintain focus on moving subjects effectively. This is crucial for sports and action photography, where subjects may change speed and direction rapidly.

- **AF Modes**:
    - Photographers can select different autofocus modes (e.g., **Servo AF** for continuous focus tracking) to suit their shooting style and subject matter, ensuring optimal focus during bursts.

3. Customizable Shooting Settings

- **Shooting Modes**:
    - The EOS R7 supports various shooting modes, allowing users to choose the best one for their needs. For example:
        - **High-Speed Continuous Shooting Mode**: For capturing rapid sequences.
        - **Low-Speed Continuous Shooting Mode**: For more controlled shooting.
- **Custom Functionality**:
    - Users can customize the camera settings to suit specific shooting scenarios, such as adjusting AF sensitivity, burst rate, and exposure settings. This customization ensures that photographers can adapt quickly to changing environments.

4. Buffer Capacity and Image Processing

- **Large Buffer Size**:
    - The EOS R7 is designed with a large buffer capacity, allowing it to handle extended bursts of high-speed shooting without slowing down. This means photographers can shoot continuously for longer periods without experiencing a drop in performance.
- **Image Processing**:
    - The camera's DIGIC X image processor plays a crucial role in maintaining high-speed shooting performance. It enables rapid processing of images, allowing for quicker write speeds to the memory card and ensuring that the camera is ready for the next shot almost instantly.

5. Memory Card Considerations

- **Fast Memory Cards**:
    - To take full advantage of the high-speed shooting capabilities, using high-speed UHS-II SD memory cards is recommended. These cards support faster write speeds, allowing for quick saving of images during continuous shooting.

6. Practical Applications of High-Speed Shooting

- **Sports Photography**:
    - Capture decisive moments in fast-paced sports, such as a soccer player kicking a ball or a sprinter crossing the finish line.

- **Wildlife Photography**:
    - Document fleeting moments in nature, like a bird taking flight or animals in motion.

- **Action Shots**:
    - Freeze action in various scenarios, from children playing to vehicles racing, ensuring sharp and dynamic imagery.

High-Speed Shooting on the Canon EOS R7 is a powerful feature that enables photographers to capture fast-moving subjects with precision. With impressive burst rates, advanced autofocus performance, and customizable settings, the R7 is well-equipped for sports, wildlife, and action photography.

By understanding and utilizing these capabilities, photographers can enhance their ability to capture stunning, dynamic images that convey movement and emotion.

Customizable Function Buttons

Customizable Function Buttons are a valuable feature of the Canon EOS R7, allowing photographers to tailor the camera controls to their specific needs and shooting preferences. This customization enhances workflow efficiency and provides quick access to frequently used settings, making it easier to adapt to different shooting situations.

Here's a detailed overview of the customizable function buttons on the R7.

1. Overview of Custom Function Buttons

- **Definition**:
    - Custom function buttons are specific buttons on the camera body that can be programmed to perform various functions or access specific settings. This allows users to streamline their shooting experience by minimizing menu navigation.

- **Pre-Assigned Functions**:
    - By default, certain buttons on the EOS R7 are assigned to specific functions, such as **ISO**, **AF-ON**, or **white balance**. However, users have the flexibility to reassign these buttons to suit their individual shooting styles.

2. Available Customization Options

- **Customizing Buttons**:
    - The EOS R7 offers various buttons that can be customized, including:
        - **Top and Rear Dials**: These can be programmed to adjust settings like aperture, shutter speed, and exposure compensation.
        - **AF-ON Button**: Can be reassigned to control functions like metering modes or drive modes.
        - **Function (Fn) Buttons**: These buttons can be customized to access features like video recording, focus modes, or other frequently used settings.
- **Menu Access**:
    - Users can assign functions that allow for quicker access to menu settings, such as changing autofocus modes, selecting shooting modes, or adjusting exposure settings without having to navigate through the main menu.

3. How to Customize Function Buttons

- **Accessing the Custom Function Menu**:
    - To customize the buttons, users can navigate to the **Custom Function** menu in the camera settings. Here, they will find options to assign specific functions to the various customizable buttons.
- **Step-by-Step Customization**:

1. **Turn on the Camera**: Make sure the camera is powered on.
2. **Access the Menu**: Press the **MENU** button.
3. **Navigate to Custom Functions**: Go to the **Custom Functions** section.
4. **Select a Button to Customize**: Choose the button you want to customize from the list.
5. **Assign a Function**: Select the desired function from the available options and confirm the selection.
6. **Save Settings**: Exit the menu, and the changes will be saved automatically.

4. Benefits of Customizable Function Buttons

- **Enhanced Workflow**:
    - By customizing function buttons, photographers can streamline their workflow, allowing for quicker adjustments while shooting. This is particularly useful in dynamic shooting environments where time is of the essence.

- **Improved Accessibility**:
    - Frequently used functions are easily accessible at the press of a button, reducing the need to navigate through menus. This enhances usability, especially for complex tasks like adjusting focus or exposure settings.

- **Personalized Experience**:
    - Customization allows users to tailor the camera to their unique shooting styles, making it feel more intuitive and user-friendly. Photographers can set the camera to work the way they do, improving overall comfort during shoots.

5. Practical Applications

- **Sporting Events**:
    - Photographers can assign functions to quickly change burst modes or adjust autofocus settings, ensuring they can capture fast-moving action effectively.

- **Portrait Photography**:
    - Custom buttons can be set for changing focus points or white balance quickly, helping to maintain the desired look while shooting.

- **Wildlife Photography**:
    - Customizing buttons for quick access to settings like exposure compensation or ISO allows photographers to adapt to rapidly changing lighting conditions in outdoor settings.

The Customizable Function Buttons on the Canon EOS R7 provide photographers with the flexibility to enhance their shooting experience. By allowing users to assign frequently used functions to specific buttons, the R7 streamlines workflow and improves accessibility, making it easier to adapt to different shooting environments.

Understanding how to effectively customize these buttons can significantly elevate your photography, allowing you to capture stunning images with greater efficiency and ease.

CHAPTER TEN
CONNECTIVITY AND SHARING OPTIONS

Wi-Fi and Bluetooth Setup

The Canon EOS R7 is equipped with both Wi-Fi and Bluetooth connectivity options, allowing photographers to easily share images, control the camera remotely, and transfer files without the need for cables. Here's a detailed guide on setting up Wi-Fi and Bluetooth on the EOS R7, along with their benefits and usage.

1. Wi-Fi Setup

- **Purpose**:
    - Wi-Fi connectivity on the EOS R7 enables users to transfer images to compatible devices (such as smartphones, tablets, or computers) and remotely control the camera using Canon's mobile applications.

- **Setting Up Wi-Fi**:

1. **Turn on the Camera**: Make sure the EOS R7 is powered on.

2. **Access the Menu**: Press the **MENU** button on the back of the camera.

3. **Navigate to Wireless Communication Settings**: Find the **Wi-Fi/Bluetooth** settings in the menu.

4. **Enable Wi-Fi**: Select the option to enable Wi-Fi. You may be prompted to create a connection.

5. **Choose Connection Method**: The camera offers various connection methods:
    - **Direct Connection**: Connect directly to a smartphone or tablet without a router.
    - **Access Point Connection**: Connect through a Wi-Fi router or access point for greater range and stability.

6. **Network Selection**: If using an access point, select the network you want to connect to and enter the password if required.

7. **Connection Confirmation**: Once connected, the camera will display a confirmation message.

- **Using Wi-Fi with Canon Apps**:
    - Download the **Canon Camera Connect app** from your device's app store. This app allows you to control the camera remotely, view and transfer images, and adjust settings from your mobile device.

2. Bluetooth Setup

- **Purpose**:
    - Bluetooth connectivity provides a low-energy option for quick image transfers and remote camera control, ideal for geotagging images and maintaining a constant connection with mobile devices.

- **Setting Up Bluetooth**:

1. **Power on the Camera**: Ensure the EOS R7 is on.
2. **Access the Menu**: Press the **MENU** button.
3. **Navigate to Wireless Communication Settings**: Go to the **Wi-Fi/Bluetooth** menu.
4. **Enable Bluetooth**: Turn on the Bluetooth setting.
5. **Pairing the Device**:
    - Open the Bluetooth settings on your smartphone or tablet.
    - Look for the camera in the list of available devices (it will usually appear as **Canon EOS R7**).
    - Select the camera to initiate the pairing process. You may need to confirm a pairing code that appears on both devices.
6. **Connection Confirmation**: Once paired, the camera will indicate a successful Bluetooth connection.

3. Benefits of Wi-Fi and Bluetooth Connectivity

- **Easy Image Sharing**:
    - Quickly transfer images to your smartphone or tablet for instant sharing on social media or cloud storage.

- **Remote Control**:
    - Use your mobile device to remotely control the camera, adjust settings, and trigger the shutter, which is particularly useful for group shots or wildlife photography.

- **Geotagging**:
    - Automatically geotag images using your smartphone's location services, providing context and details for your photography.

- **Firmware Updates**:
    - Easily update the camera's firmware via Wi-Fi, ensuring you have the latest features and improvements.

4. **Practical Tips**

- **Battery Life**:
    - Using Wi-Fi and Bluetooth can drain the camera's battery more quickly. Ensure your battery is charged, especially during extended shooting sessions.

- **Range and Connectivity**:
    - Wi-Fi provides a greater range compared to Bluetooth. For file transfers and remote shooting, ensure you are within a reasonable distance from your device.

- **Network Security**:
    - When using access point connections, ensure you are connecting to secure networks to protect your data.

The Wi-Fi and Bluetooth setup on the Canon EOS R7 enhances the camera's versatility, allowing for seamless image sharing, remote control, and geotagging capabilities. By following the setup procedures outlined above, photographers can take full advantage of these connectivity features, improving their workflow and expanding their creative possibilities.

Understanding how to effectively use Wi-Fi and Bluetooth will help maximize the potential of the EOS R7, making photography more efficient and enjoyable.

Connecting to Smartphones (Canon Camera Connect App)

The Canon Camera Connect App allows you to connect your Canon EOS R7 to your smartphone for seamless image transfer, remote shooting, and camera control. This guide will walk you through the steps to connect your EOS R7 to your smartphone using the Canon Camera Connect app, along with its features and benefits.

1. **Downloading the Canon Camera Connect App**

- **Availability**:
    - The Canon Camera Connect app is available for both **iOS** and **Android** devices.

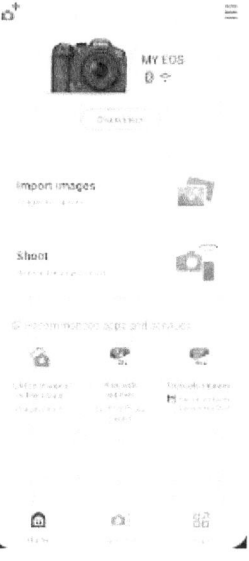

- **Installation**:
  - Go to the **Apple App Store** or **Google Play Store**, search for "Canon Camera Connect," and download the app.

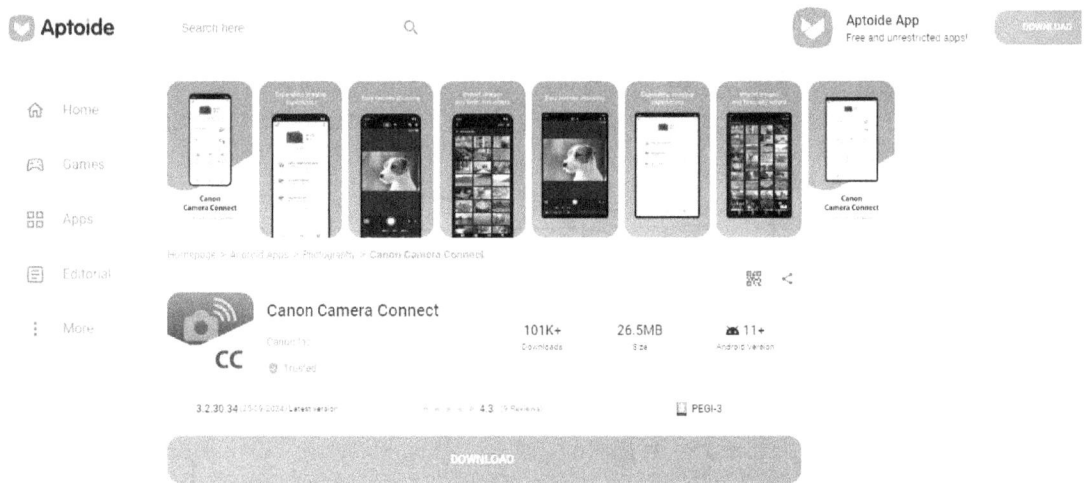

2. Preparing the Camera for Connection

- **Power On the Camera**:
  - Turn on your **Canon EOS R7**.
- **Enable Wi-Fi**:
  - Access the menu by pressing the **MENU** button.
  - Navigate to **Wireless Communication Settings** and enable **Wi-Fi**.
- **Set Up Wi-Fi Connection**:
  - Choose between **Direct Connection** or **Access Point Connection**:
    - **Direct Connection**: Connect directly to your smartphone without a router.
    - **Access Point Connection**: Connect through a Wi-Fi router for more stability.
- **Select Connection Method**:
  - For direct connections, select the **Smartphone** option, and the camera will generate an SSID (Wi-Fi name) and password.

3. Connecting the Smartphone to the Camera

- **Open Wi-Fi Settings**:
  - On your smartphone, go to **Settings** > **Wi-Fi**.

- **Join the Camera Network**:
    - Look for the SSID displayed on the camera and connect to it by entering the password if prompted.

4. Launching the Canon Camera Connect App

- **Open the App**:
    - Launch the Canon Camera Connect app on your smartphone.
- **Connect to Camera**:
    - Tap on the **Connect to Camera** option within the app.
    - The app should automatically recognize the EOS R7 connected to your smartphone.
- **Confirm Connection**:
    - Follow any prompts to confirm the connection. Once connected, you will see the camera status on the app interface.

5. Features of the Canon Camera Connect App

- **Image Transfer**:
    - Easily transfer photos and videos from your EOS R7 to your smartphone for quick sharing on social media or cloud storage.
- **Remote Shooting**:
    - Use your smartphone to remotely control the camera. You can adjust settings such as ISO, shutter speed, and aperture, and trigger the shutter from your device.
- **Live View**:
    - Access a live view of what the camera sees, making it easier to compose shots from a distance.
- **Camera Settings**:
    - Change various camera settings directly from the app, such as shooting modes, focus modes, and image quality.
- **Firmware Updates**:
    - Check for and install firmware updates directly through the app, ensuring your camera is up-to-date with the latest features and improvements.

6. **Troubleshooting Connection Issues**

- **Connection Problems**:
    - If the camera does not connect, ensure that Wi-Fi is enabled and the correct SSID is selected on the smartphone.
    - Restart both the camera and smartphone and try reconnecting.
- **Battery Considerations**:
    - Using the app can drain the camera's battery more quickly. Ensure that your battery is sufficiently charged, especially for extended use.
- **Forget Network**:
    - If issues persist, you can "forget" the camera's network in your smartphone's Wi-Fi settings and try reconnecting.

Connecting your Canon EOS R7 to your smartphone using the Canon Camera Connect app enhances your photography experience by providing quick access to images, remote shooting capabilities, and easy camera control.

By following the setup steps outlined above, you can take full advantage of these features, making your photography workflow more efficient and enjoyable. Understanding the app's capabilities will allow you to leverage your EOS R7's connectivity options, opening up new creative possibilities.

File Transfer and Remote Shooting

The Canon EOS R7 offers powerful features for file transfer and remote shooting via the Canon Camera Connect app. This functionality allows photographers to efficiently manage their images and control their camera remotely, enhancing their shooting experience.

Here's a comprehensive guide on how to transfer files and use remote shooting features with the EOS R7.

1. File Transfer

- **Purpose**:
    - File transfer enables users to quickly move images and videos from the EOS R7 to a smartphone or tablet for sharing, editing, or backup.
- **Transferring Files Using the Canon Camera Connect App**:

1. **Connect Your Smartphone to the Camera**:
    - Ensure the EOS R7 is powered on and connected to your smartphone via Wi-Fi, following the steps outlined in the previous section.
2. **Open the Canon Camera Connect App**:
    - Launch the app on your smartphone.
3. **Select Image Transfer Option**:

- In the app, tap on **Images on Camera**. This will display the images stored on the camera's memory card.

4. **Choose Images to Transfer**:
    - Browse through your images and select the ones you want to transfer. You can often choose multiple images or select all for transfer.

5. **Initiate Transfer**:
    - Tap on the **Download** or **Transfer** button to begin the file transfer. The selected images will be saved to your smartphone's gallery or designated storage area.

- **Supported File Formats**:
    - The Canon Camera Connect app supports various file formats, including JPEG and RAW images. However, note that transferring RAW files may take longer due to their larger size.

2. Remote Shooting

- **Purpose**:
    - Remote shooting allows users to control the EOS R7 from their smartphone, providing the ability to compose shots, adjust settings, and take photos without physically touching the camera.

- **Using the Remote Shooting Feature**:

1. **Connect Your Smartphone**:
    - Ensure that your smartphone is connected to the EOS R7 via Wi-Fi, as described in the previous sections.

2. **Open the Canon Camera Connect App**:
    - Launch the app and select the **Remote Shooting** option.

3. **Access Live View**:
    - The app will display a live view of the camera's sensor, allowing you to see what the camera is capturing in real-time.

4. **Adjust Camera Settings**:
    - Use the app to change various settings, such as:
        - **Shooting Mode**: Select from modes like Single Shot, Continuous Shooting, or Self-Timer.
        - **ISO**: Adjust the ISO sensitivity.
        - **Aperture**: Change the aperture value (if applicable).

- **Shutter Speed**: Modify the shutter speed.
- **Focus**: Tap on the screen to set the focus point or use manual focus if desired.

5. **Capture Images**:
   - Once you have composed the shot and adjusted the settings, press the shutter button within the app to capture the image. The photo will be taken using the camera, and you can view it instantly in the app.

- **Self-Timer and Interval Shooting**:
    o The remote shooting feature also allows you to use the self-timer for delayed shots and interval shooting for capturing sequences of images at set intervals.

3. Benefits of File Transfer and Remote Shooting

- **Efficiency**:
    o Quickly transferring files to your smartphone saves time and allows for immediate sharing on social media or cloud services.
- **Versatility**:
    o Remote shooting enables creative opportunities, such as capturing group shots without needing someone behind the camera or photographing wildlife without disturbing the subject.
- **Convenience**:
    o The ability to adjust settings remotely provides convenience, especially in challenging shooting conditions or when using a tripod.

4. Tips for Effective Use

- **Stable Connection**:
    o Ensure a stable Wi-Fi connection between the camera and smartphone for uninterrupted file transfer and remote shooting.
- **Battery Management**:
    o Using Wi-Fi for file transfer and remote shooting can drain the camera's battery. Ensure your battery is fully charged before extended use.
- **Regular Updates**:
    o Keep the Canon Camera Connect app updated to ensure compatibility with your camera and access the latest features.

The file transfer and remote shooting capabilities of the Canon EOS R7 significantly enhance the overall photography experience. By using the Canon Camera Connect app, photographers can easily transfer images, control the camera remotely, and adapt to various shooting scenarios with greater flexibility. Understanding and utilizing these features will elevate your photography, making it more efficient and enjoyable.

CHAPTER ELEVEN
MAINTENANCE AND TROUBLESHOOTING

Cleaning the Camera Sensor and Lenses

Maintaining your Canon EOS R7 by keeping its sensor and lenses clean is essential for optimal performance and image quality. Dust, fingerprints, and smudges can affect image clarity and result in unwanted artifacts. Here's a comprehensive guide on how to properly clean the camera sensor and lenses.

1. Cleaning the Camera Sensor

- **Why Clean the Sensor?**
    - The sensor collects dust and debris, which can show up as spots or blemishes in your images, especially in large areas of uniform colour, like skies.

- **When to Clean the Sensor**:
    - Clean the sensor if you notice dust spots in your images or after changing lenses in a dusty environment.

- **Cleaning Tools Needed**:
    - **Sensor Cleaning Kit**: This typically includes:
        - **Sensor Cleaning Swabs**: Designed to fit the sensor size.
        - **Sensor Cleaning Solution**: Specifically formulated for camera sensors.
        - **Blower**: To remove loose dust particles.

- **Step-by-Step Cleaning Process**:

1. **Prepare the Environment**:
    - Work in a clean, dust-free environment. Avoid windy areas or places with lots of debris.

2. **Turn Off the Camera**:
    - Power off the EOS R7 to avoid any accidental exposure to the sensor during cleaning.

3. **Remove the Lens**:
    - Detach the lens from the camera body to access the sensor. Hold the camera body facing downward to prevent any dust from settling on the sensor.

4. **Use a Blower**:
    - Use a blower to gently blow air onto the sensor. This can help remove any loose dust particles. Avoid using your mouth, as moisture can damage the sensor.

5. **Apply Cleaning Solution to Swab**:
    - Moisten a sensor cleaning swab with a few drops of the sensor cleaning solution. Do not soak it.

6. **Clean the Sensor**:
    - Gently swipe the moistened swab across the sensor in one direction (e.g., left to right), applying light pressure. Do not go back and forth; use a new swab if you need to clean again.

7. **Inspect the Sensor**:
    - After cleaning, check the sensor for any remaining dust spots. If necessary, repeat the cleaning process with a new swab.

8. **Reattach the Lens**:
    - Once the sensor is clean, reattach the lens to protect the sensor from dust.

2. Cleaning the Lenses

- **Why Clean the Lenses?**
    - Dirty lenses can lead to blurred images, reduced contrast, and colour casts. Regular cleaning helps maintain image quality.

- **When to Clean the Lenses**:
    - Clean lenses when they appear dirty or have fingerprints, smudges, or dust particles.

- **Cleaning Tools Needed**:
    - **Lens Cleaning Solution**: Use a solution specifically designed for camera lenses.
    - **Microfiber Cloth**: A soft, lint-free cloth to avoid scratches.
    - **Lens Brush**: A soft brush for removing dust.
    - **Lens Cleaning Wipes**: Pre-moistened wipes specifically for camera lenses (optional).

- **Step-by-Step Cleaning Process**:

1. **Assess the Lenses**:
    - Examine the front and rear elements of the lens to determine the level of dirt or smudging.

2. **Remove Dust with a Brush**:
    - Use a lens brush to gently sweep away any loose dust or debris. Be careful not to scratch the glass.

3. **Apply Lens Cleaning Solution**:
   - Lightly spray a few drops of lens cleaning solution onto a clean microfiber cloth (never directly onto the lens).

4. **Wipe the Lens**:
   - Use the microfiber cloth to gently wipe the lens in a circular motion, starting from the centre and moving outward. This helps avoid streaks.

5. **Repeat if Necessary**:
   - If stubborn smudges remain, repeat the cleaning process with a fresh section of the cloth or a new cloth.

6. **Clean the Rear Element**:
   - Don't forget to clean the rear element of the lens in the same manner as the front element, as it can also affect image quality.

3. General Tips for Maintenance

- **Avoid Touching the Lens**:
  - Always handle the lens by the edges to minimize the risk of fingerprints and smudges.

- **Use a UV Filter**:
  - Consider using a UV filter to protect the lens from scratches and dirt. This can make cleaning easier.

- **Regular Checks**:
  - Regularly inspect both the sensor and lenses, especially before important shoots, to ensure they are clean and ready for use.

- **Professional Cleaning**:
  - If you are uncomfortable cleaning the sensor yourself or if there are persistent spots that won't come off, consider taking your camera to a professional service for cleaning.

Cleaning the camera sensor and lenses of your Canon EOS R7 is crucial for maintaining image quality and ensuring optimal performance. By following the steps outlined above and using the appropriate tools, you can keep your equipment in excellent condition and capture stunning images without unwanted artifacts. Regular maintenance will prolong the life of your camera and lenses, enhancing your overall photography experience.

Firmware Updates

Keeping your Canon EOS R7 firmware updated is essential to ensure optimal performance, access to new features, and overall camera reliability. Firmware updates can fix bugs, improve compatibility with lenses and accessories, and enhance functionality. This guide provides a comprehensive overview of how to check for and perform firmware updates on your EOS R7.

1. Understanding Firmware Updates

- **What is Firmware?**
    - Firmware is the software that controls your camera's hardware. It is embedded in the camera's memory and manages the device's operations, features, and performance.

- **Importance of Updates**:
    - Updates may include improvements in autofocus performance, image processing, menu options, bug fixes, and compatibility with new lenses.

2. Checking the Current Firmware Version

Before performing an update, it's essential to know your camera's current firmware version:

1. **Turn on the Camera**:
    - Power on your EOS R7.

2. **Access the Menu**:
    - Press the **MENU** button on the back of the camera.

3. **Navigate to the Firmware Version**:
    - Go to the **Setup Menu** (wrench icon).
    - Scroll down and select **Firmware version**.

4. **View the Firmware Version**:
    - The current firmware version for the camera body and any attached lenses will be displayed. Take note of the version number.

3. Preparing for the Firmware Update

- **Required Items**:
    - A fully charged battery for the camera.
    - An SD card formatted in the camera (make sure to back up any important data).
    - A computer with internet access to download the firmware.

- **Backup Important Data**:
    - Before updating, back up any critical images or settings to avoid potential data loss.

4. Downloading the Firmware Update

1. **Visit the Canon Support Website**:
    - Go to the official **Canon USA** or your regional Canon support website.

2. **Find Your Camera Model**:
    - Search for "Canon EOS R7" in the support section to access the product page.

3. **Locate Firmware Updates**:
    - Navigate to the **Drivers & Downloads** section.
    - Find the latest firmware update available for the EOS R7.

4. **Download the Firmware**:
    - Download the firmware file (usually in ZIP format) to your computer.
    - Extract the ZIP file to access the firmware file, which typically has a .FIR extension.

5. Installing the Firmware Update

1. **Insert the SD Card**:
    - Insert the formatted SD card into your computer.

2. **Transfer the Firmware File**:
    - Copy the firmware file (.FIR) onto the root directory of the SD card (do not place it in any folders).

3. **Safely Eject the SD Card**:
    - Safely eject the SD card from your computer and insert it back into the camera.

4. **Update Firmware**:
    - Power on the camera and press the **MENU** button.
    - Go to the **Setup Menu** (wrench icon).
    - Select **Firmware version**.
    - The camera will detect the firmware file on the SD card. Follow the on-screen prompts to start the firmware update process.

5. **Follow Instructions**:
    - Confirm that you want to proceed with the update. The camera will display progress bars indicating the update status.
    - Do not turn off the camera or remove the SD card during the update process, as this could cause damage to the firmware.
6. **Completion**:
    - Once the update is complete, the camera will restart automatically.
    - Check the firmware version again to confirm that the update was successful.

6. Post-Update Steps

- **Reset Settings (if needed)**:
    - After the update, you may want to reset camera settings to factory defaults or adjust them based on your preferences.
- **Check for Compatibility**:
    - Test the camera's performance with lenses and accessories to ensure everything works as expected after the update.
- **Consult Release Notes**:
    - Review the release notes or update details provided on the Canon website to familiarize yourself with any new features or changes.

Regularly updating the firmware of your Canon EOS R7 is crucial for maintaining optimal camera performance and access to new features. By following the steps outlined in this guide, you can easily check for updates, download the latest firmware, and install it safely.

Staying up-to-date with firmware will enhance your photography experience and help you make the most of your camera's capabilities.

Common Errors and How to Fix Them

Like any advanced camera, the Canon EOS R7 may encounter various errors or issues during use. Understanding these common errors and their solutions can help you troubleshoot effectively and maintain a smooth shooting experience. Below is a guide on some of the most common errors, along with steps to resolve them.

1. Error Messages

- **"Err 01: Communication between the camera and lens is faulty."**
    - **Cause**: This error occurs when there is a communication issue between the camera body and the lens.

- **Fix**:
    1. Remove the lens from the camera body.
    2. Clean the lens contacts (the metal pins on the lens and the camera) with a soft, dry cloth.
    3. Reattach the lens securely.
    4. If the error persists, try using a different lens to determine if the issue is with the lens or the camera body.

- **"Err 02: Memory card error."**
  - **Cause**: This indicates a problem with the memory card, such as corruption or improper insertion.
  - **Fix**:
    1. Turn off the camera and remove the memory card.
    2. Check the card for damage or dirt. Clean the card's contacts with a soft, dry cloth.
    3. Reinsert the memory card securely.
    4. If the error persists, try formatting the card in the camera (back up any important files first) or replacing the card.

- **"Err 30: Shutter error."**
  - **Cause**: This error occurs when there is a problem with the camera's shutter mechanism.
  - **Fix**:
    1. Turn off the camera and remove the battery for a few minutes.
    2. Reinsert the battery and turn the camera back on.
    3. If the error persists, consult a professional technician or Canon service centre for repairs.

2. Battery and Power Issues

- **Camera Won't Turn On**
  - **Cause**: This may be due to a depleted battery, improper battery installation, or battery contacts.
  - **Fix**:
    1. Check the battery level and charge it if necessary.
    2. Ensure the battery is properly seated in the camera.

3. Clean the battery contacts with a dry cloth.
- **"Battery Communication Error"**
    - **Cause**: This indicates an issue with the battery, such as incompatibility or a faulty battery.
    - **Fix**:
        1. Remove the battery and reinsert it.
        2. Check for any damage or dirt on the battery contacts.
        3. If using a third-party battery, switch to the original Canon battery to see if the error persists.

3. Image Quality Issues

- **Blurry Images**
    - **Cause**: Blurriness can result from camera shake, incorrect focus, or a dirty lens.
    - **Fix**:
        1. Ensure you are using a fast enough shutter speed to prevent motion blur, especially at longer focal lengths.
        2. Use image stabilization (if available) or a tripod for stability.
        3. Check your focus settings and ensure the camera is focusing correctly on the subject.
        4. Clean the lens to remove any dirt or smudges that could affect image quality.

- **Poor Low-Light Performance**
    - **Cause**: Low-light conditions can lead to grainy images if the ISO is set too high.
    - **Fix**:
        1. Adjust the ISO settings to find a balance between exposure and noise.
        2. Use a larger aperture to allow more light in.
        3. Experiment with longer exposure times while using a tripod to stabilize the camera.

4. Connectivity Issues

- **Wi-Fi or Bluetooth Connection Failure**
    - **Cause**: This can occur due to settings issues, software conflicts, or signal interference.

- Fix:
    1. Ensure that the camera's Wi-Fi/Bluetooth is enabled in the settings.
    2. Restart both the camera and the smartphone or device you are trying to connect to.
    3. Remove the connection on the smartphone and re-establish it by following the pairing process in the Canon Camera Connect app.
    4. Move closer to the Wi-Fi source to eliminate signal interference.

5. Menu and Settings Problems

- **Camera Settings Resetting**
    - **Cause**: Settings may reset due to a drained battery or if the camera is turned off for an extended period.
    - **Fix**:
        1. Check the battery condition and ensure it is fully charged.
        2. Save your custom settings in the camera's menu to easily restore them after a reset.

- **Menu Unresponsive**
    - **Cause**: The camera menu may become unresponsive due to a software glitch.
    - **Fix**:
        1. Turn off the camera and remove the battery for a few minutes.
        2. Reinsert the battery and power the camera back on.
        3. If the problem persists, consider performing a factory reset in the menu settings.

The Canon EOS R7 is a sophisticated camera, but like any electronic device, it can experience common errors and issues. By understanding these potential problems and their solutions, you can troubleshoot effectively and continue capturing great images.

Regular maintenance and familiarity with your camera's features will help minimize issues and enhance your photography experience. If you encounter persistent problems that you cannot resolve, consult the user manual or contact Canon customer support for assistance.

CHAPTER TWELVE
TIPS AND TRICKS FOR BETTER PHOTOGRAPHY

Shooting in Low Light Conditions

Shooting in low light conditions can be challenging, but the Canon EOS R7 is equipped with features that make it capable of capturing high-quality images even in dim environments. This guide provides tips and techniques to optimize your photography when light is limited.

1. Understanding Low Light Conditions

- **Definition**: Low light refers to environments with insufficient natural or artificial light, such as during twilight, indoors, or on cloudy days.

- **Challenges**: The main challenges of low-light photography include motion blur, noise (graininess), and difficulty in achieving accurate focus.

2. Utilizing Camera Settings

- **Increase ISO Sensitivity**:
  - The EOS R7 has a native ISO range of 100 to 32,000, expandable to 51,200.
  - Increasing the ISO allows the camera to be more sensitive to light, helping to achieve proper exposure in low light.
  - **Tip**: Start with a lower ISO setting and gradually increase it to find the best balance between exposure and noise.

- **Open the Aperture**:
  - Use a wider aperture (smaller f-number) to allow more light to hit the sensor.
  - Lenses with a large maximum aperture (e.g., f/1.8, f/2.8) are ideal for low-light photography.
  - **Tip**: Use Aperture Priority mode (Av) to easily control aperture settings.

- **Slow Down the Shutter Speed**:
  - A slower shutter speed allows more light to enter the camera. However, be cautious, as it can introduce motion blur if the camera or subject moves.
  - Use a tripod or stabilize the camera to minimize blur.
  - **Tip**: Experiment with different shutter speeds, but remember to keep it above the reciprocal of the focal length (e.g., for a 50mm lens, use at least 1/50s) to avoid camera shake.

3. Leveraging Autofocus Techniques

- **Use Manual Focus**:
    - In low light, autofocus systems may struggle to lock on. Switch to manual focus for better control, especially with stationary subjects.
    - Use the camera's focus peaking feature to assist in achieving precise focus.

- **Enable Low-Light AF**:
    - The EOS R7 features Dual Pixel Autofocus, which performs well in low light. Ensure that low-light AF assist is enabled in the settings.
    - **Tip**: Use the camera's built-in LED light (if available) or an external light source to aid focusing in very dark environments.

4. Stabilization Techniques

- **In-Body Image Stabilization (IBIS)**:
    - The EOS R7 includes IBIS, which compensates for camera shake and allows for sharper images at slower shutter speeds.
    - **Tip**: Combine IBIS with lens stabilization (if available) for maximum stability.

- **Use a Tripod or Monopod**:
    - A tripod provides the best stability for long exposures. If a tripod isn't available, a monopod or resting the camera on a solid surface can help.

5. Post-Processing Considerations

- **Shoot in RAW**:
    - Capturing images in RAW format allows for more flexibility in post-processing, particularly with exposure adjustments and noise reduction.
    - **Tip**: Use software like Adobe Lightroom or Canon's Digital Photo Professional to edit RAW files and enhance low-light images.

- **Noise Reduction**:
    - Apply noise reduction techniques during post-processing, particularly if you had to use high ISO settings. Most editing software provides noise reduction filters to clean up images.

6. Practical Tips for Low Light Shooting

- **Plan Your Composition**:
  - Scout your location beforehand, if possible. Look for interesting light sources or compositions that can enhance your low-light images.

- **Use Continuous Shooting Mode**:
  - If you are shooting moving subjects, use burst mode to increase the chances of capturing a sharp image, as it can help you get the right moment with better exposure.

- **Experiment with Light Sources**:
  - Utilize available light sources creatively, such as streetlights, candles, or reflections, to add depth and interest to your photos.

- **Practice**:
  - Low-light photography often requires experimentation. Take your time to try different settings and techniques to see what works best for your style and the specific conditions.

The Canon EOS R7 is equipped with advanced features that make it suitable for low-light photography. By understanding and utilizing its capabilities—such as increasing ISO, adjusting aperture, using manual focus, and stabilizing your shots—you can capture stunning images in challenging lighting conditions. With practice and experimentation, you'll enhance your skills and feel more confident shooting in low light.

Using Filters and Effects

Filters and effects are powerful tools that can enhance your photography by altering the way light interacts with your lens and adding creative flair to your images. The Canon EOS R7 offers various ways to incorporate filters and effects, both physically and digitally. This guide explores the types of filters available, their uses, and how to apply effects in-camera or during post-processing.

1. Types of Filters

- **Polarizing Filters**:
  - **Function**: Reduces reflections and glare from surfaces such as water and glass, enhances colours, and increases contrast.
  - **Use**: Ideal for landscape photography, allowing for deeper blues in the sky and more vibrant greens in foliage.
  - **Tip**: Rotate the filter while looking through the viewfinder or LCD to see the effect in real-time.

- **Neutral Density (ND) Filters**:
    - o **Function**: Reduces the amount of light entering the lens, allowing for longer exposure times without overexposing the image.
    - o **Use**: Great for achieving motion blur in flowing water or creating a sense of movement in still scenes.
    - o **Tip**: Use ND filters in bright conditions when you want to shoot with wide apertures or slow shutter speeds.
- **Graduated Neutral Density (GND) Filters**:
    - o **Function**: Similar to ND filters but with a gradient effect, allowing for selective light reduction across the frame.
    - o **Use**: Useful for balancing exposure in scenes with a bright sky and darker foregrounds.
    - o **Tip**: Position the gradient line according to your horizon line to achieve the best effect.
- **UV Filters**:
    - o **Function**: Originally used to block UV light, these filters now primarily serve to protect the lens from scratches and dust.
    - o **Use**: Always a good practice to keep a UV filter on your lens for protection, especially in outdoor environments.
- **Special Effects Filters**:
    - o **Function**: These can create unique looks, such as soft focus, starbursts, or colour effects.
    - o **Use**: Explore creative photography by using these filters for portraits or artistic shots.

2. Using Filters with the Canon EOS R7

- **Attaching Filters**:
    - o Ensure you choose the right size filter for your lens. Filters can be attached via screw mount (filter thread) or through a filter holder system.
    - o Align the filter correctly and twist it onto the lens until it's secure.
- **Checking for Vignetting**:
    - o When using wide-angle lenses or stacking multiple filters, watch for vignetting (dark corners) in your images.
    - o If vignetting occurs, consider using slimmer filters or adjusting your composition.

3. In-Camera Effects

The Canon EOS R7 offers various in-camera effects that can be applied directly to images:

- **Creative Filters**:
    - The camera has built-in creative filters, such as "Miniature," "Fish Eye," and "Grainy Black and White," which can be applied to images.
    - Access these through the camera's menu under the "Shooting" or "Creative" settings.

- **Picture Styles**:
    - Use Picture Styles to adjust colour tones, contrast, and sharpness.
    - Common styles include Standard, Portrait, Landscape, and Neutral, each affecting how colours are rendered in your images.
    - You can create custom Picture Styles for specific shooting conditions.

4. Post-Processing Effects

In addition to in-camera effects, post-processing offers even more flexibility and creative options:

- **Software Options**:
    - Use photo editing software like Adobe Lightroom, Photoshop, or Canon's Digital Photo Professional to apply filters and effects digitally.

- **Applying Effects**:
    - Experiment with adjustments such as contrast, saturation, and clarity to enhance your images.
    - Explore presets or plugins that mimic the look of physical filters (e.g., ND effects or vintage film looks).

- **Layering Techniques**:
    - In software like Photoshop, use layers to selectively apply effects to specific areas of your image (e.g., using a mask with a gradient to simulate a GND filter).

5. Tips for Using Filters and Effects

- **Experiment and Practice**:
    - Take time to experiment with different filters and effects to understand their impact on your images.
    - Keep a record of settings and techniques that yield good results for future reference.

- **Know Your Scene**:
    - Consider the lighting, subject matter, and mood you want to convey when choosing filters and effects.
    - Some filters are better suited for specific genres, such as landscapes or portraits.
- **Keep it Simple**:
    - While filters and effects can enhance your images, avoid overusing them. Sometimes, subtle changes yield the best results.

Using filters and effects with the Canon EOS R7 can significantly enhance your photography and help you achieve your creative vision. By understanding the types of filters available, how to use them effectively, and exploring in-camera and post-processing options, you can elevate your images and expand your artistic capabilities.

Whether you're capturing landscapes, portraits, or artistic shots, filters and effects can be valuable tools in your photography toolkit.

Composing Shots with the Rule of Thirds

The Rule of Thirds is one of the fundamental principles of photography composition that can significantly enhance the visual appeal of your images. It helps create a balanced and dynamic composition, guiding the viewer's eye and making your photos more engaging. Here's a comprehensive guide on how to apply the Rule of Thirds using your Canon EOS R7.

1. Understanding the Rule of Thirds

- **Concept**: The Rule of Thirds divides the frame into a grid of nine equal parts, created by two horizontal lines and two vertical lines. The idea is to place the most important elements of your scene along these lines or at their intersections, known as "power points."
- **Purpose**: This technique helps create tension, energy, and interest in the composition, leading to a more aesthetically pleasing photograph.

2. How to Use the Rule of Thirds

- **Enabling the Grid Display**:
    - To help visualize the Rule of Thirds while composing your shots, enable the grid feature in the Canon EOS R7.
    - Go to the **Menu**, navigate to the **Display Settings**, and turn on the grid overlay. This will help you see the thirds as you frame your subject.
- **Positioning Key Elements**:
    - Place the subject or focal point of your shot along one of the grid lines or at one of the intersections.

- For example, if you're photographing a person, position their eyes along the top horizontal line.

3. Practical Applications

- **Landscapes**:
  - For landscape photography, align the horizon with one of the horizontal lines. If the sky is more interesting, place the horizon lower, giving it more space. If the foreground is more compelling, position the horizon higher.

- **Portraits**:
  - When composing a portrait, place the subject's eyes on one of the top intersections. This draws attention to the face and creates a more engaging image.

- **Architecture**:
  - In architectural photography, align vertical lines of the building with the vertical grid lines to create a sense of stability and balance.

- **Action Shots**:
  - In action photography, such as sports, position the subject along a vertical line with space in the direction they are moving. This creates a sense of motion and anticipation.

4. Experimenting Beyond the Rule of Thirds

- **Breaking the Rule**:
  - While the Rule of Thirds is a helpful guideline, don't be afraid to break it when it serves your creative vision. For example, centering a subject can create a strong impact in certain compositions, especially in minimalist photography.

- **Combining with Other Techniques**:
  - Use the Rule of Thirds in conjunction with other compositional techniques, such as leading lines, framing, or symmetry, to enhance your photographs further.

5. Practicing the Rule of Thirds

- **Take Multiple Shots**:
  - Experiment with different compositions by adjusting your subject's position relative to the grid. Take multiple shots from varying angles to see how the Rule of Thirds influences the final image.

- **Analyse Your Images**:
    - Review your photos to see how the Rule of Thirds affected the composition. Consider which images stand out and why, and adjust your technique based on your observations.

6. Final Tips for Using the Rule of Thirds

- **Be Mindful of Backgrounds**:
    - Ensure that the background complements your subject and doesn't distract from it. The Rule of Thirds can help you position subjects against cleaner backgrounds.

- **Use Natural Frames**:
    - Look for natural frames in your environment, such as trees, windows, or doorways, to add depth to your composition while applying the Rule of Thirds.

- **Practice, Practice, Practice**:
    - The more you practice using the Rule of Thirds, the more instinctive it will become. Over time, you'll develop an eye for effective compositions that elevate your photography.

The Rule of Thirds is a valuable compositional technique that can enhance the visual impact of your photographs with the Canon EOS R7. By understanding its principles, applying them thoughtfully, and experimenting with your compositions, you can create more engaging and dynamic images.

Remember, while the Rule of Thirds is a helpful guideline, the most important aspect of photography is to express your unique perspective and creativity.

Mastering Portraits, Landscapes, and Macro Photography

The Canon EOS R7 is a versatile camera well-suited for a variety of photography styles, including portraits, landscapes, and macro photography. Each genre has its own techniques and settings to achieve stunning results. Here's a comprehensive guide to mastering these three photography styles.

1. Mastering Portrait Photography

Portrait photography focuses on capturing the personality and mood of an individual or group. The EOS R7's features make it a powerful tool for creating beautiful portraits.

Essential Techniques

- **Choose the Right Lens**:
    - Use a lens with a wide aperture (e.g., 50mm f/1.8 or 85mm f/1.8) to achieve a shallow depth of field, blurring the background and emphasizing the subject.

- **Use Natural Light**:
    - Take advantage of natural light by positioning your subject near windows or outdoors during the golden hour (the hour after sunrise or before sunset) for soft, flattering light.
- **Focus on the Eyes**:
    - Ensure that the subject's eyes are in sharp focus. The EOS R7's Dual Pixel Autofocus is excellent for tracking eyes, especially when using Eye Detection AF.

Camera Settings

- **Aperture Priority Mode (Av)**:
    - Use Aperture Priority mode to control the depth of field. A wide aperture (e.g., f/2.8) isolates the subject from the background.
- **Shutter Speed**:
    - Keep the shutter speed fast enough to avoid motion blur, typically 1/200s or faster, especially for moving subjects.
- **ISO Settings**:
    - Adjust the ISO according to the lighting conditions. Keep it as low as possible to minimize noise while ensuring a well-exposed image.

2. Mastering Landscape Photography

Landscape photography captures the beauty of nature and scenery. The EOS R7's high-resolution sensor and dynamic range make it ideal for this genre.

Essential Techniques

- **Use a Tripod**:
    - A sturdy tripod is essential for stabilizing your camera during long exposures, especially in low-light conditions or when shooting at smaller apertures.
- **Compose with Foreground Interest**:
    - Include elements in the foreground to create depth and lead the viewer's eye into the scene.
- **Utilize Leading Lines**:
    - Use natural lines (like rivers, paths, or roads) to draw attention to your subject and create a sense of direction.

Camera Settings

- **Aperture**:
  - Use a smaller aperture (e.g., f/8 to f/16) for greater depth of field, ensuring that both the foreground and background are in focus.

- **Shutter Speed**:
  - Depending on the scene, use longer exposures to capture motion in elements like water or clouds. Utilize ND filters if necessary to reduce light and achieve longer exposures.

- **ISO Settings**:
  - Keep the ISO low (100-400) to minimize noise, especially in detailed landscape shots.

3. Mastering Macro Photography

Macro photography involves capturing small subjects at close range, revealing intricate details often missed by the naked eye. The EOS R7 excels in this area with its excellent autofocus capabilities.

Essential Techniques

- **Use a Macro Lens**:
  - Invest in a dedicated macro lens (e.g., Canon RF 100mm f/2.8L Macro IS) to achieve true macro capabilities and capture fine details.

- **Stabilization**:
  - Use a tripod or a stabilizer to avoid camera shake. Consider using the EOS R7's In-Body Image Stabilization (IBIS) for handheld shooting.

- **Focus on Details**:
  - Pay attention to composition, lighting, and background. Isolate your subject by using a blurred background (bokeh effect).

Camera Settings

- **Aperture**:
  - Use a wider aperture (e.g., f/2.8 to f/5.6) to achieve a shallow depth of field, focusing on specific details of the subject while blurring the background.

- **Shutter Speed**:
  - Use a faster shutter speed to freeze motion, especially for subjects like insects. A speed of at least 1/200s is recommended.

- **ISO Settings**:
    - Adjust ISO according to lighting conditions, but try to keep it low to avoid noise, especially when capturing fine details.

The Canon EOS R7 is a powerful tool for mastering various photography styles, including portraits, landscapes, and macro photography. By understanding the essential techniques and camera settings for each genre, you can capture stunning images that highlight your unique perspective. Practice regularly, experiment with different settings, and don't hesitate to step outside your comfort zone to enhance your skills and creativity in photography.

THANK YOU FOR READING

www.ingramcontent.com/pod-product-compliance
Lightning Source LLC
Chambersburg PA
CBHW062108220526
45471CB00010B/3653